Stamping Fun

for Beginners

NORTH LIGHT BOOKS
CINCINNATI, OHIO
www.artistsnetwork.com

Other fine North Light Books are available from your local bookstore, art supply store or direct from the publisher.

09 08 07 06 05   5 4 3 2 1

Library of Congress Cataloging-in-Publication Data

McGraw, MaryJo.

  Stamping fun for beginners / by MaryJo McGraw.

    p. cm.

  Includes index.

  ISBN 1-58180-585-3 (pbk. : alk. paper)

  1. Rubber stamp printing. I. Title

TT867.M39 2005

761--dc22

2004057569

fw

F+W PUBLICATIONS, INC.

Interior stamp designs: LL865 Tiny Trimmings stamps by Hero Arts; F-1668 Spiral stamp by A Stamp In The Hand Co.

Editors: Jolie Lamping Roth, Jennifer Fellinger
Designer: Marissa Bowers
Layout Artist: Jessica Schultz
Production Coordinator: Robin Richie
Photographer: Christine Polomsky, Tim Grondin, Al Parrish
Photo Stylist: Jan Nickum

METRIC CONVERSION CHART

TO CONVERT	TO	MULTIPLY BY
Inches	Centimeters	2.54
Centimeters	Inches	0.4
Feet	Centimeters	30.5
Centimeters	Feet	0.03
Yards	Meters	0.9
Meters	Yards	1.1
Sq. Inches	Sq. Centimeters	6.45
Sq. Centimeters	Sq. Inches	0.16
Sq. Feet	Sq. Meters	0.09
Sq. Meters	Sq. Feet	10.8
Sq. Yards	Sq. Meters	0.8
Sq. Meters	Sq. Yards	1.2
Pounds	Kilograms	0.45
Kilograms	Pounds	2.2
Ounces	Grams	28.35
Grams	Ounces	0.035

About the Author

MaryJo McGraw is a nationally known rubber stamp artist and author whose work has been featured in leading rubber stamp enthusiast publications. Innovative techniques and creative teaching methods have made her a much sought-after instructor at conventions, retreats, cruises and stores for more than fifteen years.

Acknowledgments

To William and Darlene of Stampland, the folks from whom I bought my first stamp those many years ago. Thank you for inspiring tens of thousands—perhaps millions—with the love of rubber stamps!

To the gang at North Light. As always, their energy and excitement are what keep me heading on to the next book. Thanks to Jolie Lamping Roth for signing on as original editor. Jolie, you are incomparable and I will miss you. To Jennifer Fellinger for finishing up with the grunt work at the end. What a pleasure you have been to work with! To Christine Polomsky, my photographer, you are the best and I love how you make it so easy! As always, Tricia Waddell, you are an inspiration. Thanks!

To all the companies who have supported me with friendship and products through the years, especially JudiKins, Carmen's Veranda, Rubbermoon, Art Gone Wild!, Postmodern Design, Hero Arts and my good friends at CoffeeBreak Design—thank you, thank you, thank you! Your constant support means so much.

Dedication

To my dear friend, Elaine Madrid, who really gave me my start in the business. Thank you for all the wonderful years of fun, friendship and adventures down the rubber road.

TABLE OF Contents

27 TECHNIQUES & PROJECTS 36

Introduction

I used to be into dolls—fashion dolls, cloth dolls, porcelain dolls, you name it. It was something of an obsession. I went to doll shows with my mom in the late 1970s and early 1980s. Once in a while, there would be a nice couple selling rubber stamps at these shows. I was intrigued. Rubber stamps? Did people really buy these?

There had to be at least five hundred stamps on their table, and the vast array of images on those little wood blocks amazed me. And so, I bought my very first stamp, an image of a little fairy standing next to a tall flower. As I purchased the stamp, I thought, "This is great. I can stamp this image on all my stationery." I could not wait to get home and start stamping! Little did I know how this one stamp would change the course of my life.

Before I knew it, I had a shoebox filled with stamps, and I was hunting down any bit of information I could find on rubber stamps, stamp stores and sources for supplies. Every year it seemed that my collection would double. Within ten years I had over ten thousand stamps—all loved, some used, many never even touched! Today, my collection of stamps is always in flux. I still buy new ones every year and keep the old ones that hold senti- mental value, and I also trade some stamps and give others away. I have found that ten thousand stamps is too many, but three thousand is a manageable number.

So much for my dolls, which at this moment are boxed away in the basement. Stamps are my obsession now. I will not say that everyone will fall under the spell of stamps, and I won't claim that one stamp will change your life. My love of stamps coincided with a life- long love of art, and I came to envision stamps as incredible tools for creating art. Some people see stamps as things to collect, while others regard stamps as crafter's tools, a means to create usable items like greeting cards. There is no right or wrong reason for indulging in a little stamping fun, and whatever your reason, you can be sure that stamps will make you a more creative person.

Getting Started

I believe all beginner stampers should start out on the right foot. After years of stamping and teaching, I am always disappointed to see how many new stampers eagerly spend money on a load of products they do not know how to use. If you are just beginning to discover the joys of stamping, I have one bit of advice: *Take classes!* The information you receive in classes, whether it comes from the teacher or from your fellow students, is invaluable. And, when you learn which products you really do not need, the money that you save will more than pay for the classes.

With such a wide selection of rubber stamps available today, you may wonder which are the best stamps to buy as a beginner. Invest in simple graphic designs such as swirls, stars and hearts. These designs are versatile and can be used year after year with trendy stamps, cute images or arty collage. You'll tend to keep these functional designs long after you dump the stamps you bought in your first year.

It also pays to invest in alphabet stamps. If you are a beginner, start with a set of small, basic alphabet stamps. When it comes to making cards and gifts, the ability to create your own text is essential. You'll find that a few well-designed alphabets can be lifesavers. The big plus is that these stamps are not just useful for composing text; they can be used to create background designs, too. But be forewarned: Alphabet stamps alone can become an obsession!

When you are considering a new stamp design, ask yourself a few questions about the design. Do I really love this stamp or am I buying it because it is a popular image? Can I use this image for more than one style of greeting? Is this a design that has many applications? In other words, can it be used as a background, as a single image or as a means to invent another look?

With this book, a few basic supplies and a bit of enthusiasm, you are about to have some stamping fun!

The following list is my personal top ten list of stamping supplies—other than stamps, of course—that you need to have:

1 A good craft knife with a soft grip or a retractable knife
2 A transparent ruler with a metal edge
3 A self-healing cutting mat
4 An embossing heat gun
5 Clear embossing powder
6 One black dye ink pad
7 One black pigment ink pad
8 One black solvent ink pad
9 One clear embossing ink pad
10 Great paper

Tools & Materials

Once you have started your stamp collection, you may wonder what other tools and supplies you'll need for stamping. I'll offer a practical tip: Buy tools and materials that you can use in many craft and art projects, not just stamping.

Tools

Listed on this and the following page are some of the most common tools used for rubber stamping techniques. There are many stamping tools available, but these are the tried-and-true ones that I use on a regular basis.

Tools for Working with Paper

A craft knife is one of the most important tools in a stamper's kit. Not only do I use the blade for cutting but I also use the back of the blade for scoring and creasing paper. There are many styles of craft knives available today. I prefer a knife with a no. 11 blade and a soft grip handle. There are also retractable penknives, which are very safe. Change the blades often for clean, easy cutting and a professional look.

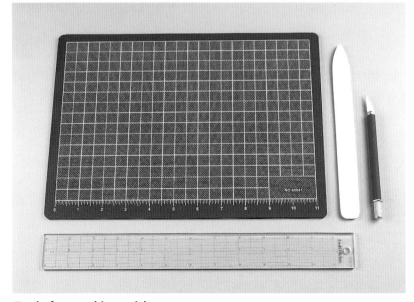

Tools for working with paper
A self-healing cutting mat, bone folder, craft knife and transparent ruler are musthaves for cutting and working with paper.

A transparent ruler with an embedded metal edge is ideal for craft use. (A quilter's ruler, though transparent, does not have the metal edge.) I always use a C-Thru ruler, which features grid lines on the clear, plastic surface. The ½" (13mm) markings are perfect for working with paper since most card sizes are designed in ½" (13mm) increments.

A self-healing cutting mat, a must-have for the serious stamper, will keep your papercrafts from slipping while being trimmed or cut. It also saves knife blades from constant wear and breakage.

A bone folder is a smooth tool shaped like a letter opener and made out of bone (hence the name), wood or resin. The bone folder is a bookbinder's tool, used to score and crease papers. I prefer it for creasing paper rather than scoring since it leaves a wide score mark rather than a crisp one. Many stampers have a selection of bone folders in several sizes.

Tools for Rubber Stamping

A heat gun is a necessary tool for embossing techniques. There are many models available, all ranging in price and complexity. It is wise to buy a lower-priced gun until you determine what type you really need. The heat from the gun is intense, so if you have young children, look for a model that looks the least like a hair dryer.

Color dusting brushes are inexpensive miniature stippling brushes—great tools for applying paints, chalks, inks and more on paper.

Brayers make it easy to ink both paper and stamps, especially large stamps, quickly and evenly. They are indispensable tools if you stamp with paints and heavy pigment inks. I recommend a good 4" (10cm) soft rubber brayer that is detachable from the handle.

Makeup sponges, or cosmetic sponges, are inexpensive and easily found. Perfect for applying color to many different surfaces, these sponges can create several color effects on paper, ranging from a soft pastel look to an intensely colored airbrush look.

Linoleum cutters, specifically made for printmaking, are a necessity for rubber stampers who enjoy cutting their own designs. You can use linoleum cutters to carve and cut designs into a variety of surfaces, including plastic, linoleum and rubber.

Tools for rubber stamping
A rubber stamper's kit often includes (clockwise from top left) makeup sponges, color dusting brushes, a heat gun, a linoleum cutter and a brayer.

RUBBER BRUSHES: Another Useful Tool

Rubber brushes are rubber-tipped tools that can be used to work chalk into a surface. Because they leave little or no residue, they are more effective than a cotton swab or makeup applicator. Rubber brushes can also be used for creating patterns in thick layers of paint or ink. They are easily cleaned with a wet wipe or paper towel.

Materials

There are so many materials that can be used in rubber stamping, the list could go on and on. I'm limiting this list to the basic materials, but feel free to develop your own list of "must-have" materials as you explore rubber stamping. Be sure to check the materials list that precedes every project in this book, as some of the objects may not be discussed in this section.

Stamps

The stamper's most essential tool is, of course, the rubber stamp itself! Rubber stamps come mounted and unmounted. For beginners, I do not suggest starting with unmounted stamps, even though they are a good option for a tight budget and limited storage space. Speaking from years of experience, I bet you'll use your mounted stamps more since they are ready to go. If you do buy unmounted stamps, I have one suggestion: Mount them immediately! To this day, I have tons of unmounted stamps still waiting to be mounted.

For mounted stamps, there are generally three main components. The first, the *mount*, can be one of any number of materials, including wood, acrylic, foam or clay. A well-made hardwood mount is the best choice for collectors and regular stampers. Wood holds up well under extreme use and is the perfect surface for beautiful indexing (see *Indexing*, page 13).

The second component, the *cushion*, is the foam between the mount and the rubber die. Good cushion affects how well a stamp prints and how long the stamp lasts. Red rubber makes the best and longest-lasting cushion, but because most stamp companies cannot afford its expense, a sticky gray or black cushion is often used instead. This gray or black cushion is good, but it tends to shrink with age. When buying stamps, look carefully at how the cushion is trimmed; it should not be undercut or smaller than the rubber die. If you are mounting your own stamps, use red rubber cushion.

The third component, the *rubber die*, is the most important part of the stamp. I only recommend rubber, as it is tough and virtually eternal. In the long run, cheap stamps just aren't worth it. While great for a quick image, stamps with foam dies and clear (polymer) dies are easily damaged and won't withstand the test of time.

To find quality rubber stamps, check out stamp stores in your area. You can purchase general supplies and basic materials in addition to rubber stamps at many scrapbook and craft stores. For inspiration, attend stamping and scrapbooking conventions, where you'll see the newest ideas and hottest trends in rubber stamping. Finally, explore stamping and crafting Web sites to discover the many resources available online.

Inks

Inks can be categorized into three basic groups: dye, pigment and solvent. Some techniques require certain types of ink, while others are compatible with any kind of ink. As you gain stamping experience, you'll become familiar with the characteristics and uses of each ink.

Dye ink is usually the first type of ink a stamper buys. It has a transparent look on coated and uncoated papers, including vellum. Dye inks, which dry through evaporation, dry easily and quickly on most paper. For this reason, they are not good for embossing. Dye inks are typically packaged in white solid-topped cases, with the color of ink represented on the top or side of the case. Today's dye ink is generally presented in a raised foam pad or on a raised linen-covered felt. Raised pads are usable on every size stamp, making them the best long-term purchase.

Inks and stamp cleaners
Become acquainted with the different kinds of stamping inks and stamp cleaners.

Pigment ink is sold in clear-topped cases, allowing you a view of the ink's true color. This type of ink has a thicker, more opaque appearance and is now available in several textures, including regular, pearl/metallic and chalk. Regular pigment ink features a smooth, soft texture. Metallic and pearlized pigments have a gritty texture with a beautiful sheen, a result of the ground mica infused in the ink. Chalk pigment has a chalky, very matte finish. Pigment inks, which come on raised foam pads, dry slowly by being absorbed into the paper surface. This slow process makes pigment inks ideal for embossing. When not embossed, these inks do not dry well on slick, coated surfaces. However, there are some newly-developed pigment inks that can be set with a heat gun on any surface.

Solvent ink is made to be used on nonporous surfaces, such as acetate, glass, ceramic and plastic. They are also the perfect lightfast, fadeproof and waterproof ink for paper. Solvent inks, like dye inks, dry by evaporation. Included in this category are alcohol inks, like Piñata Colors and the newer Adirondack alcohol inks, as well as many fabric inks. You can buy solvent inks bottled with a blank pad, bottled with no pad or in a solid case on a linen-covered raised pad.

Other inking supplies, such as markers and paints, can also be used to ink stamps. Because it is important that the ink on the stamp be wet, I like to use "juicy" markers with ink that stays wet.

INDEXING

Indexing is the stamp image that appears on top of the mount, used as a means to identify the stamp design. Some indexing utilizes a suggested coloring of the image. Plain black indexing is the norm and is preferred by purists since it shows the true design.

Stamp Cleaners

Cleaning your rubber stamp is necessary when you change from a dark to a light ink or from pigment ink to solvent ink. For this task, choose a good solvent cleaner with a scrub top. This one type of cleaner can handle all types of inks and paints. It also removes the silicone on most new rubber stamps, which makes the stamp accept its first inking better. You can also use plain water, baby wipes or even alcohol to clean many products from your stamps, but only solvents will remove everything. I recommend using cleaners that contain conditioners, which keep the stamp surface soft and pliable.

Paper

The first thing that people usually notice on a greeting card is the paper. If you want that first impression to be a good one, seek out the best quality paper for your stamping projects. Flimsy or cheap paper won't cut it!

For greeting cards in particular, I prefer heavyweight cardstock, which comes coated and uncoated. Coated stocks are generally smooth to the touch and can be glossy or matte. There are even pearlized, glittered and shimmering coated cardstocks. Inks and paints tend to sit on the surface of coated papers. Consequently, they are not ideal for pigment inks, which dry by absorbing into the paper. Uncoated cardstock has a more toothy feel, with a surface that inks and paints sink into.

Uncoated paper can be found in a variety of surfaces. Some, like the surface of watercolor paper, are plain, while others feature a texture or a pattern, such as linen or bamboo. Textured cardstock is often difficult to stamp on, so it typically serves better as an underlayer for a layered card than as a stamping surface.

Translucent vellum is a sheer paper with a matte surface. Available in many weights and colors, vellum has an elegant appearance. There is also a variety of plastic papers that resemble vellum but feel slick and look more modern; many of these plastic papers can be stamped.

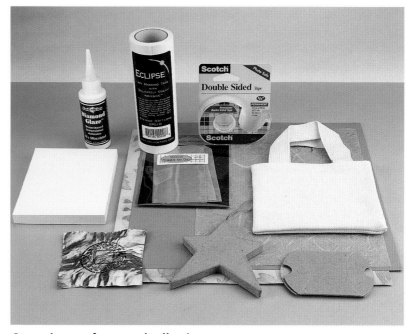

Stamping surfaces and adhesives
Stamping possibilities seem endless with the paper and adhesives available today.

Adhesives

Dimensional adhesive, such as Diamond Glaze water-based dimensional adhesive (my favorite adhesive medium), is perfect for all kinds of stamping projects because it is extremely versatile and can be mixed with an array of inks, paints, pigments and dyes. When a thin coating is brushed onto paper, Diamond Glaze can be used as a basic glue. It can also be used as a heavy adhesive for three-dimensional embellishments. Because it remains clear when dry, Diamond Glaze is great for collage and découpage, for shiny nonporous surfaces like mica tiles, acetate, beads and glitter, and as a fixative over chalk, watercolor and crayons.

Tape, especially double-sided, or double-stick, tape, comes in handy for many stamping projects. I use double-sided tape for most paper-to-paper applications and layering techniques. My favorite is Mosaic Tape from JudiKins, a very strong, double-sided, paper-lined tape that can be torn, cut and easily heated. Several brands of clear double-sided tape will work well for projects using sheer paper, such as vellum. And for those times when you could use an extra hand, keep a roll of removable masking tape close by!

Art masking tape, which comes in rolls, is delicately sticky and removable. Eclipse art tape is the product I rely on for the technique of masking. Some people use self-adhesive notes or just plain thin paper with a bit of repositionable glue for masking.

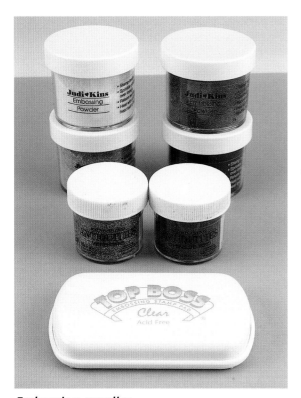

Embossing supplies
Embossing powders and embossing inks create fantastic stamping effects.

Embossing Supplies

Embossing powders are applied to wet ink on paper, then set with a heat gun. The powders come in many colors and textures, but clear embossing powder is essential because it can be used with all kinds of colors and inks, especially pigment inks. Embossing powder is available in three weights: detail weight, which is excellent for fine lines; regular or standard weight, which is used most frequently in color mixes; and thick weight, which is typically used for heavy layering techniques.

Clear embossing ink pads were developed specifically for embossing. The glycerin-based ink dries slowly, allowing time for the embossing powder to be applied and to set. Embossing ink can be used on many surfaces, including metal, wood and several kinds of paper. Some embossing inks are slightly tinted, so you can see your stamp design before embossing it.

Other Supplies

Markers, colored pencils and chalk can all be used to color stamped images. You can achieve a wide variety of color effects with these products, ranging from soft and subtle to saturated and intense. Each product has its own characteristics, so experiment with them a bit to see which look you like best.

Foil leafing pens allow you to edge, touch up and decorate paper and embellishments. These pens work on paper, cardstock, cardboard and nonporous surfaces. When several layers are applied, they truly create the look of metal. Other types of paint pens will work, but they will not have the same rich look.

Powdered pigments are raw pigments containing mica, which creates a pearlized effect. To adhere the powder to the surface of the paper, a binder such as embossing ink, glue or spray fixative is needed. Pigment powders can be mixed with a wide range of stamping products. My favorite pigment powders are Pearl Ex.

White carving blocks are the perfect medium for creating your own stamps. These blocks hold their shape and do not break down with use. White plastic and pink rubber erasers can also be used. Do not use gum erasers because they break down too easily.

Water brushes, shaped like pens with a durable nylon tip, contain cartridge reservoirs that can be filled with water or any other liquid. You can then apply water onto a surface through the tip, mixing it with a variety of mediums, including paint, pencil and crayon. Water brushes make it possible to highlight, shade or blend color over stamped images. These brushes produce the same look as a paintbrush, but allow you more control of the water flow. Be aware that price does not dictate the brush quality. More expensive brushes have a flow constrictor, a tiny piece of plastic with a small hole that controls the water flow through the reservoir. It keeps the water in the brush clean and restricts the flow out of the brush. Cheaper brushes do not have this constrictor, which makes them better for working with glue and thick paint.

A water spritzer is a pump spray bottle that can be used to mist the surface of rubber stamps. Rubber stamping companies produce spritzing bottles, but you can simply fill a small, clean spray bottle with water.

Other supplies
To give your stamping projects a unique touch, you can use many additional materials, such as (clockwise from top right) powdered pigments, foil leafing pens, markers, chalks and pastels, carving blocks, colored pencils, water brushes and water spritzers.

Embellishments

Embellishments are a fun and easy way to dress up any card or papercraft. With them, you can add a final touch or a finishing detail to pull the entire design together. The best part about choosing embellishments is that you can be as unique and creative as you want!

These days, card makers, stampers and scrapbookers have access to a seemingly endless selection of embellishments and accents. Consider both thickness and weight when you choose your embellishment items. I suggest looking for flat items no thicker than ¼" (6mm). If you plan to mail your embellished card, keep in mind that extra bulk will often increase the cost of postage.

There is a wide assortment of embellishments available at scrapbook and stamping supply stores. You can find premade decorated tags, metal frames and alphabets, pewter stickers, fabric papers and so much more—it is almost mind-boggling. Don't limit yourself to just these specialty shops, however. Thrift and antique stores are excellent haunts for buttons, beads, fabric trims, ribbons, old postcards, photos, keys and bottle caps. Hardware stores also provide great inspiration for embellishments. Look for wire, washers, O-rings, glass cut to size, address stickers, metal house numbers, paint chips and sheet metals. And don't forget to search your own attic or basement, where you might find a surprising stash of little treasures that offer great embellishing possibilities!

MICRO GLAZE: Another Useful Material

An excellent fixative for many surfaces, this super fine wax is a good choice for many mixed media projects. It can be mixed with powdered pigments and be buffed into paper and other surfaces. Micro Glaze is a great resist wax to use with paints and inks, since it leaves no oil residue on paper and the excess can be buffed away once the color has dried.

Techniques

Because this book is for beginners, I've devoted a large introductory section to the basic techniques of stamping. In the following pages, you'll find techniques for basic stamping, working with paper, applying color to stamped images, adding details to stamped projects and fixing mistakes. When you feel comfortable enough to move on to the projects, you can use this section as a handy resource.

Inking Stamps with an Ink Pad

When I first started stamping, there was a rule: Do not rock the stamp! Because the excess rubber around the dies was not trimmed well, rocking left ink marks on the paper. Today, rubber is so well trimmed that you can rock the stamp all you want. Be aware, however, that pressing a stamp onto a surface as hard as you can does not produce a better result. A slight rocking motion is fine for larger stamps, but in general, firm, even pressure is the way to go.

To apply ink most effectively, tap the stamp onto the stamp pad gently and rapidly. Resist the urge to press the stamp into the pad with full force, as this inks the recessed areas that should remain uninked.

1 With a rapid, gentle tapping motion, press the stamp into the ink pad.

2 With firm, even pressure, press the inked stamp onto the paper.

3 When stamping a background pattern, aim for a continuous and random application, like a patterned fabric, for a more professional look. Rotate the stamp a quarter turn after each stamp to vary the orientation of the image, and allow the stamping to run off the edges of the paper. To stamp off the edge, place a paper towel under the paper.

More Ways of Inking Stamps

Think beyond the ink pad! There are so many ways of inking stamps other than with an ink pad. Paints, markers and other types of inks can all be used on stamps. Any type of water-soluble paint can be applied to a stamp with a brayer, and colors from a delicate pad can be applied with a sponge. Many types of markers, especially markers with ink that stays very wet, can be used directly on the stamp. These inking methods allow you to selectively ink your stamp and tailor the look of the stamped image.

To create a multicolor image, use a multicolor ink pad. There is currently a wide variety of multicolor and rainbow pads on the market. Some feature removable sections that allow you to apply colors separately. Tap the ink pad straight up and down onto the stamp several times to apply the color.

Markers permit you to ink specific areas with different colors. Apply the color to the stamp, blending the colors directly on the stamp as desired. When using markers to ink a stamp, work quickly to keep the ink wet. After you've finished applying the ink, exhale a long, deep breath over the stamp surface. This will keep the moisture of the ink even. Stamp the paper.

To use a brayer for inking, first pick up ink on the brayer by rolling it across the ink pad. Then, roll the brayer across the rubber stamp until the surface is evenly inked. Brayers are especially effective tools for inking large stamp surfaces and for applying paints and heavy pigment inks to stamps.

Cleaning Stamps

My students would tell you that this is one subject I often rant about in class! Most people clean their stamps too much, as it is a common misconception that stamps require cleaning after every use. In fact, a stamp actually works better if there is a bottom coating of dry ink on it. You must clean a stamp if you are switching from dark ink to light ink or from pigment ink to solvent ink, but if you work from light to dark dyes and from solvents to pigments, your stamps will be fine.

To clean a stamp, use a solvent stamp cleaner with a scrub top. (As noted on page 14, you can also use plain water, baby wipes or alcohol to clean many products from your stamps, but only solvents will remove everything.) After applying the cleaner to the stamp, wipe the surface with a paper towel or old soft cloth.

1 Apply cleaner directly to the stamp surface.

2 Allow the cleaner to penetrate the stamp surface, then wipe the surface with a paper towel or an old soft cloth.

Cleaning and Re-inking Ink Pads

Do not panic if you accidentally get ink on your stamp pads. Most pads can be wiped clean with a paper towel. Foam pads can actually be rinsed out with water, blotted well, then re-inked. Before re-inking a foam stamp pad, swipe the dirty pad onto a piece of white cardstock to remove any grime. If the pad is still grungy after repeating this step several times, rinse out all the ink with water. Blot the pad dry and let it sit overnight, then re-ink it. When you purchase a new ink pad, it's a good idea to also buy a bottle of re-inker to keep on hand.

To remove grime from an ink pad and prepare it for cleaning, swipe the pad across a sheet of cardstock.

Preparing a New Solid Stamp

"Solid," "bold," "positive surface," "reversing block," "palette" and "shadow" are all terms for stamps that have a solid rubber surface. Today, many geometric-shaped solid stamps are referred to as shadow stamps, a term coined by Hero Arts in the late 1990s. These kinds of stamps are particularly resistant to the first application of ink because the vulcanizing process leaves a residue of silicone. To be able to ink the stamp successfully, you must first remove the silicone. A good solvent cleaner will do this quickly and easily. This preparation can be used for any stamp, but it is especially effective for solid stamps.

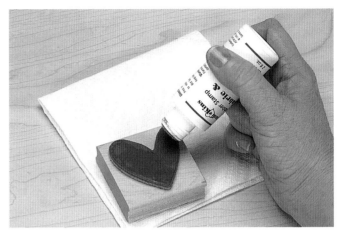

Before using a new solid stamp, clean the stamp surface with solvent cleaner to remove the silicone residue.

Stamping Borders

You can use a single stamp to create a beautiful border. This is the perfect way to make unique, personalized gift stationery. It's amazing how just one stamped border can brighten up otherwise dull correspondence. When creating borders, stamps with geometric designs work best.

1 Stamp the back flap of an envelope. If the stamp design has a definite top and bottom, make sure the stamp is oriented the correct way. Press the stamp halfway off the flap, right off the edge. Continue stamping, lining up the images corner to corner. It is fine to overlap the images a bit; just be sure to keep checking the direction of the stamp.

2 Using the same technique, stamp around the front of the envelope.

Embossing

Embossing can give the simplest image a polished, professional look, adding texture by raising the stamped image off the surface of the paper. It is the embossing technique that hooks many people on stamping.

For this technique, you must use either pigment ink or clear embossing ink with embossing powder. Use colored embossing powder with clear embossing ink and clear embossing powder with colored pigment inks. Embossing powders are available in different weights. Use detail weight powder to emboss fine lines, use regular or standard weight powder in color mixes, and use thick weight powder for embossing in heavy layers.

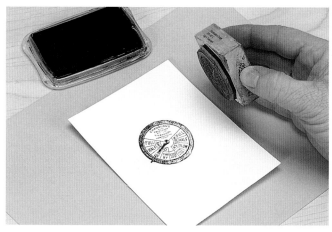

1 Ink the stamp generously with pigment ink. Press the stamp onto the paper.

2 Quickly pour embossing powder over the entire stamped image. Do not sprinkle the powder, as sprinkling takes up time during which the ink might dry.

tips Clear embossing powder is the easiest to use. Metallic powders are thicker, which make them most effective for filling up space. All colored powders are based in white, which give them a pasty appearance if they are overheated. Note that the longer colored embossing powders are heated, the lighter they become.

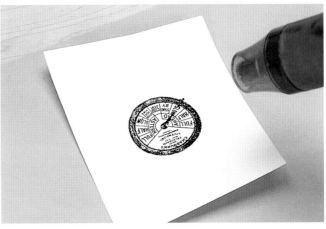

3 Remove the excess embossing powder by pouring it or tapping it off the paper. If there seems to be a lot of excess powder, hit the back of the paper firmly. If all the powder falls off, your ink was too dry.

4 Heat the powder with a heat gun, keeping the gun low to the paper, about ½"–1" (13mm–3cm) from the surface, as you move it slowly and continuously across the image. Continue heating until the embossing powder is fully cooked (see *Emboss It 'Til It's Done!*, below).

Using a Clear Embossing Pad

The VersaMark watermark pad is one of the best clear embossing pads on the market since it is a foam-based pad. Use the pad to ink the stamp, then proceed with the normal embossing technique. Or, use clear embossing ink by itself as a resist.

Ink the stamp with a clear embossing ink pad and stamp a design onto the surface, as shown. You can then emboss the stamped design, following steps 2–4, above, or you can treat the design as a resist, inking directly over it.

EMBOSS IT 'TIL ITS DONE!

If the surface of the embossing powder looks like an orange peel, it is undercooked.

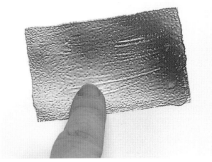

The embossing powder is fully cooked when the surface is smooth and shiny.

Using a Ruler

Using a ruler is one of the most fundamental skills for working with paper—and, luckily, one of the easiest to master. Holding the ruler correctly is important when you desire a straight line or cut, whether you are scoring or cutting the paper.

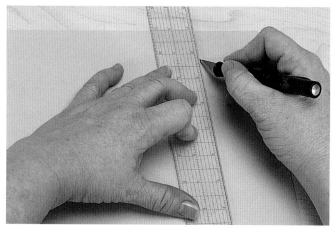

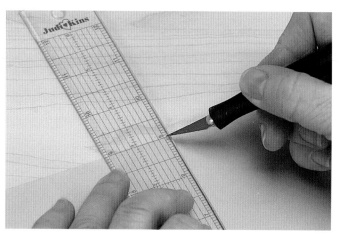

1 To hold the ruler correctly, place your ring finger and thumb on the beveled edge of the ruler, then use your forefinger and middle finger to hold the ruler in place. Use your pinky finger to balance your hand on the surface of the paper or cutting mat. Held in place like this, the ruler will not slip out from under the knife or bone folder.

2 This ruler has horizontal ½" (13mm) markings, making it easier to cut paper to specific measurements. A transparent ruler with markings eliminates the need to pencil in measurements on your paper. Many rulers feature markings as blocks, which can be used to measure in imperial or metric increments.

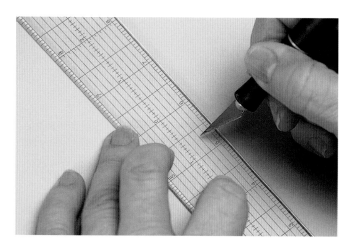

3 This ruler also has vertical ⅛" (3mm) markings, which allow you to measure increments in the opposite direction.

Scoring Paper

Learning to score your own paper has its advantages. Because you won't be limited to prescored cardstock, you will save money and increase your paper selection. Plus, you'll have the ability to customize the dimensions for your own handmade cards. You can use a bone folder or a craft knife to score paper. I prefer the crisper line that results from scoring the paper with the back of the craft knife tip.

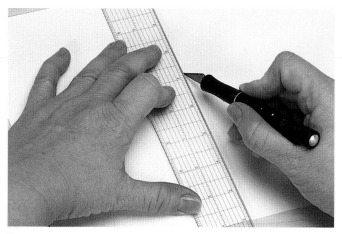

1 Position the ruler on the paper as desired, then hold it in place, as instructed on page 24. Press the back of the craft knife tip firmly to the paper, then run the knife down the metal edge of the ruler.

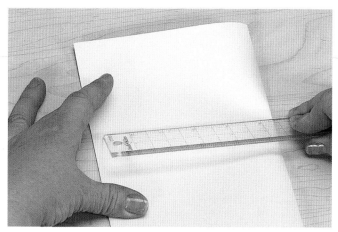

2 Fold the paper along the score line, pressing with the beveled side of the ruler to flatten the crease. I prefer to crease most papers with the score mark on the inside of the card.

3 Once the cardstock is folded, cut the card in half to create two A2 style cards, each measuring 4¼" x 5½" (11cm x 14cm).

tip An A2 card (folded) measures 4¼" x 5½" (11cm x 14cm). This is a standard measurement for greeting cards, and envelopes for this size are readily available. The card itself can easily be created by folding a standard 8½" x 11" (22cm x 28cm) sheet of cardstock in half, then cutting the folded sheet in half.

Making a Frame

With the help of a C-Thru ruler, it is not difficult to make frame cards with interior openings. When using a transparent ruler, I measure in terms of large and small blocks. The large blocks on a C-Thru ruler equal ½" (13mm) each, and the small blocks, which run perpendicular to the large blocks, equal ⅛" (3mm) each. For straight lines and right angles, use the small vertical railroad track along the metal edge as a guide. Position these "tracks" along the outside edge of the paper, then line up the horizontal lines with the ends of the paper. Cut the paper with a craft knife, using the blocks as your guide. Cut the remaining sides in the same manner.

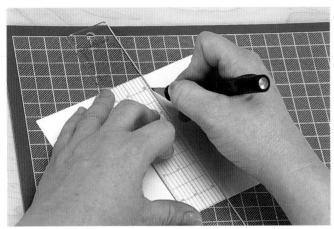

1 Score and fold a sheet of cardstock to create an A2 card. Unfold the card, then lay it on a cutting mat. Line up the ruler so its edge measures four small blocks, or ½" (13mm), in from the crease. Make sure the top edge of the card is aligned with a horizontal marking on the ruler. With a craft knife, cut along the edge of the ruler, starting the cut ½" (13mm) from the top edge.

2 Stop cutting ½" (13mm) from the bottom edge.

3 Remove the ruler. Check the cut to make sure that each end measures ½" (13mm) from the top and bottom edges.

4 Repeat the cut, this time cutting ½" (13mm) from the right edge of the paper. Start and stop the cut ½" (13mm) from the top and bottom edges, as before.

5 Line up the ruler so that its edge is ½" (13mm) from the bottom edge of the paper, at a 90° angle to the two cuts. Make a third cut, running the blade from the end of one cut to the end of the other.

6 Line up the ruler so that its edge is ½" (13mm) from the top edge of the paper, at a 90° angle to the first two cuts. Make a fourth and final cut, running the blade from the end of one cut to the end of the other.

7 Remove the interior to create a window, then refold the card.

Tearing Paper

Torn edges give rubber stamp creations an interesting look. You can use a specially made deckle ruler to create a deckle edge, or, for the same effect, you can simply place a metal-edged ruler on a sheet of paper and tear the paper swiftly along the ruler's edge. For a white or contrasting edge, tear the paper toward you. This adds a layered look to your torn paper. For a true deckle edge without the white contrast, tear the paper away from you. For easy tearing, I generally use the process shown below rather than using a ruler. First, I wet the paper where I'd like it to tear with a paintbrush, water brush or cotton swab soaked with water. Once the water has penetrated the paper, I gently pull the two sides of the paper apart without the aid of a ruler. This gives a softer torn look, exposing the fibers of the paper.

1 Stamp a design onto a page torn from a book.

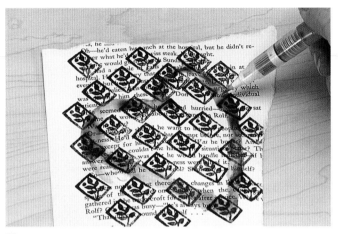

2 Use a water brush or a paintbrush to apply water to the paper in the shape of a heart.

3 Tear out the heart shape, following along the wet outline.

Coloring Stamped Images with Markers

With markers, you can add rich, intense color to the stamped image.

Color within the lines of the stamped image with markers. Avoid coloring over the lines. Always leave some white areas within the design.

TO GET RICHER COLOR

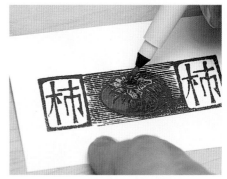

To achieve warm, rich hues, first color the area with a yellow marker. Then, add the color (here, red and green) over the yellow.

Coloring Stamped Images with Chalk

Because it is so forgiving, chalk is an excellent medium for coloring designs. If you get a smudge of chalk on the paper surface, it can be easily removed with an eraser.

Use a craft knife to scrape piles of colored chalk onto a palette. Pick up a small amount of chalk with a rubber brush, color dusting brush, sponge or another tool, then apply the chalk to the paper surface in a circular motion. Set the chalk with spray fixative or aerosol hair spray.

Coloring Stamped Images with Colored Pencil

It's easy to fall in love with the look of colored pencils. You can control the application of the color, giving the stamped image a light touch or an intense glow.

Fill in the stamped image with your choice of colored pencils. Avoid covering any of the stamped lines since the pencils can leave a chalky finish.

Using a Brayer

Brayers are wonderful tools for creating a background on paper and other stamping surfaces. You can roll out rich layers of ink and paint and alter the thickness to create a lighter or darker background. For the best results and easiest cleanup, I always use a soft brayer with a detachable handle.

1 Load the brayer by rolling it several times across the surface of the ink pad.

2 Roll the inked brayer across a sheet of paper. Continue rolling until you achieve the color intensity you desire.

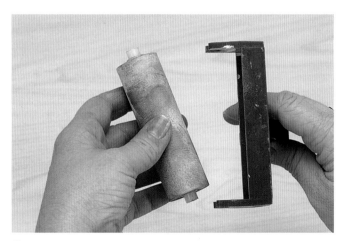

3 When you are finished, clean the roller. A detachable handle makes the task of cleaning up easy.

ANOTHER WAY OF INKING A BRAYER

Instead of rolling the brayer across the ink pad, apply the ink to the brayer directly from the pad. To do so, press the individual ink pad against the surface of the roller, covering it entirely with ink.

Stippling

Stippling provides a beautifully textured surface for your stamp designs. When stippling, it is very important to use a stiff brush, preferably made of natural hair. For a light application of ink, an uneven brush is best. For heavy stippling, a flat, even brush allows more color to be applied.

1 Load a small, stiff brush with ink and pounce it over the surface of the paper.

2 To intensify the color, pinch or wrap a rubber band around the bristles. Ink the condensed bristles, then pounce over the surface.

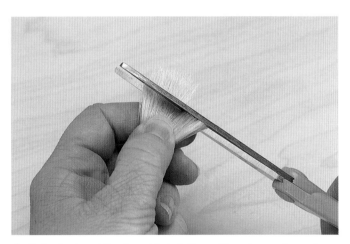

3 If desired, cut the brush's bristles with scissors to make them even stiffer.

tip

For stippling, a brush for each color is desirable. Keep one for every basic color—reds, oranges, yellows, etc. It is not necessary to have a brush for every shade.

Masking

Masking is an important technique to master, and this is one technique where practice makes perfect. With masking, you can make one stamped image appear to be behind another, adding depth and dimension to the entire composition. Always use art masking tape, such as Eclipse, or very thin paper to mask. Whether you're using tape or paper, use only a craft knife for cutting masks so that the edges are smooth and even. Cutting a mask with scissors will leave rough, uneven edges.

1 Ink the stamp and stamp the paper. Then, without re-inking, press the stamp onto the roll of art masking tape, rolling the stamp across the curved surface to get a complete image. Cut the image from the tape roll, leaving some excess.

2 Place the stamped tape on a cutting mat. Use a craft knife to carefully and cleanly cut out the stamped image, trimming right inside the perimeter line of the image. The mortise refers to the hole that is remaining in the mask. Place the mask aside.

3 Cut the image in half for two different colors, keeping the trim line clean.

4 Lay the mortise over the stamped paper, aligning the cut edges of the mask with the perimeter edges of the stamped image.

5 Add the first layer of color to the stamped image.

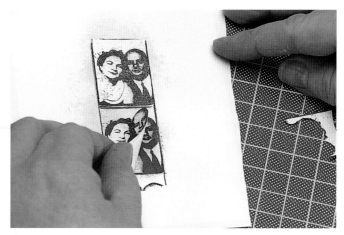

6 Take the two halves cut out in step 3. Lay one piece over the top half of the image. Cut out the background from the other piece and align it over the bottom image. The tighter and cleaner the cut, the better the result will be.

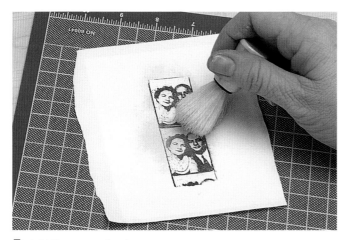

7 Add the second color.

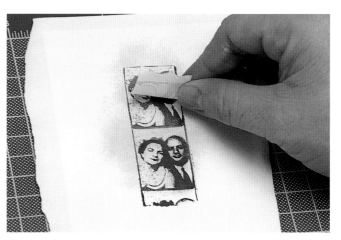

8 Remove the bottom mask and align it over the top stamped image.

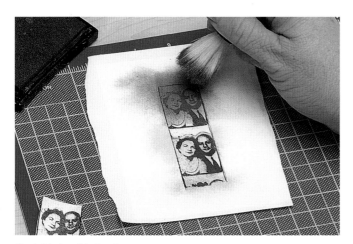

9 Add the third color.

10 Remove the mask.

Edging

For a nice finishing detail, add color to the edges of your final product. This can be done by simply inking the edge of the paper with a foam ink pad. One word of caution: Only foam ink pads are tough enough to withstand this technique.

Run the center of the foam ink pad along the edges of the paper.

Using Double-Sided Mounting Tape

For making cards and other papercrafts, I recommend using double-sided mounting tape. Double-sided tape is a great choice for greeting cards and, with a stronger hold and no drying time, it is a better option than glue. Mounting tape, unlike regular double-sided tape, typically has a foam "interior" that adds dimension by slightly lifting the adhered object off the surface. For pop-up and three-dimensional cards, you can fold the tape to increase the depth.

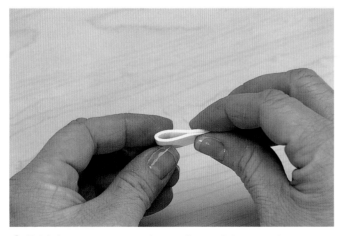

1 Fold the tape over, as shown. Cut and then stack.

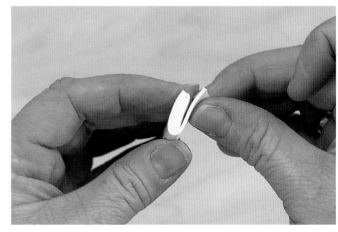

2 Roll the tape several times to increase the depth, pulling the liner as you go.

Fixing Smudges

Smudges are generally easy to remove. The following technique works best on coated paper, but it also works on uncoated paper. However, it does not work on duotone or printed paper, as you'll scrape away the color, exposing the white surface beneath.

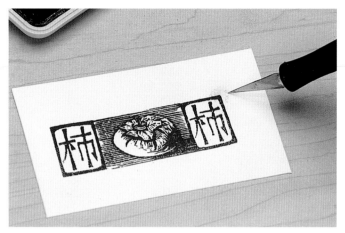

1 Gently lift the smudge with a craft knife, removing just the top layer of paper.

2 Scrape away the remaining smudge with a craft knife, using a back-and-forth motion.

3 Even out the roughness of the paper surface by gently rubbing a white plastic eraser over the area you scraped.

Fixing Misstamps

Sometimes an area doesn't print well if the stamp doesn't completely adhere to the paper. In this case, you can complete the stamped image with a marker. Permanent felt-tip marker works best for filling in black stamped areas.

Touch up misstamps with a felt-tip marker.

27 Techniques & Projects

I am a very technique-oriented paper artist, and I hope to pass this attitude on to my students and readers. I believe that learning how to do basic techniques will open up many more doors than learning how to make one specific project or work from one particular pattern. After all, if you master the basics, you'll have the know-how to complete a wide range of different projects, whether you are using a book as a guide or inventing your own.

This perspective has influenced my selection of projects for this book. The twenty-seven projects that are included in the following pages are all technique-based. In fact, I prefer that you think of these twenty-seven ideas not as projects but rather as building blocks for future stamping projects. If you learn, practice and master each of the techniques, you'll be a well-equipped rubber stamper.

Don't feel limited by the products that I use in these projects. In some cases, I do specify types of inks and paper for the best results. However, many of the stamp designs, paper patterns and ink colors, included in parentheses or in brackets, reflect my own taste as well as my favorite brands and styles. You'll soon find your own favorites, too. Feel free to experiment—play with the techniques and try different approaches. Who knows? You may discover something new and develop your own unique look.

My goal with this book is to teach you as many basic stamping methods as possible so that your stamping can be limitless. Once you have these techniques down, you will be ready to take any class, try any new method from books and magazines alike, and ultimately create your own original designs.

white cardstock

colored (lime green) cardstock

stamp | POSTMODERN FRIDA KAHLO DESIGN |

stamp cleaner and paper towel or soft cloth

felt-tip markers (several colors)

water spritzer

ruler

craft knife or bone folder

scissors

double-sided tape

Inking Stamps with Markers

For those stamps that just beg for color, markers are the perfect inking tools. Markers offer the versatility of applying color wherever you want on the stamp surface. This technique is particularly useful for floral, fauna and face stamps, since the different parts of the design can be colored separately and the colors can be blended. In this project, I used markers to ink specific parts of the stamp—the hair, the clothing and parts of the face—with just the right colors. Stamping on white paper will give you the truest and most vivid color. Moisture is the key when inking your stamp, so look for "juicy" felt-tip markers that will not dry out.

1 Color the rubber stamp with a felt-tip marker, using your choice of color for each section of the stamp. Allow the colors to dry on the stamp. Once the colors have set, reapply the color with marker.

2 Spritz the stamp very lightly with a fine mist of water. For smaller stamp designs, you can moisten the surface by exhaling a deep, even breath over the stamp.

3 Press the inked stamp onto a sheet of white cardstock.

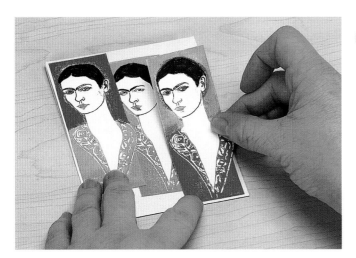

4 When you want to re-ink the stamp with different colors, clean the stamp (see *Cleaning Stamps*, page 20), then repeat steps 1–3 using other color combinations. When you have finished, cut out the stamped images.

5 Score and fold the colored cardstock to create an A2-size card. Use double-sided tape to adhere the stamped images onto the front of the card. If necessary, touch up any areas with marker.

Materials

white cardstock

colored (brown) cardstock

stamp | RUBBERMOON BEE DESIGN |

solvent or dye ink pad (black)

chalk (several colors)

elastic band

small embellishment

makeup sponge or rubber brushes

ruler

craft knife

bone folder

scissors

double-sided tape

tip The old adage "you get what you pay for" rings true when it comes to buying chalk. If you love the look of chalk, buy the best you can afford. The heavier and denser the chalk, the better the quality. Lower-quality chalk is lightweight and has many air holes, which reduce the amount of pigment it can carry. A good chalk set will last you a very long time.

Using Chalk to Color Stamped Images

If it's a soft and subtle look that you're after, try using chalk. Chalk can be easily applied over stamped images with paintbrushes, rubber brushes, makeup sponges or even your fingers. By blending chalk, you can create a beautiful background ranging from a quiet pastel tone to an intensely vivid hue. The only limitation with this technique is the kind of ink you can use; do not use pigment ink because chalk will not adhere to it.

1 Ink the stamp with solvent or dye ink, then press the stamp onto a sheet of white cardstock.

2 Use a craft knife to scrape off some chalk onto the stamped cardstock. When scraping, concentrate the chalk particles directly over the areas you want colored.

3 Blend the chalk onto the cardstock with a makeup sponge or rubber brush in a circular motion. Allow the chalk to spread beyond the perimeter of each stamped design.

tip If you're looking for more intense color, try using rubber brushes for applying and blending chalk. Rubber brushes give chalk a much richer look whereas a color dusting brush or sponge lends a lighter touch of color.

4 Add other colors, scraping chalk into the background area between each stamp. Blend the colors with a makeup sponge or rubber brush.

5 Apply additional color directly onto the paper with the tip of the chalk sticks.

6 Trim the edges of the stamped cardstock. Score and fold the colored cardstock to create a card. Use double-sided tape to attach the stamped design to the front of the card. Open up the card and lay it on a cutting mat, with the front facing up. At the center of the crease, create a small hole by gently twisting a craft knife into the paper.

7 Thread an elastic band through the hole. Stretch the band around the folded card, then secure the other end of the band through the hole. The band should be taut around the entire card. For a finishing touch, add a small embellishment to the band.

Materials

white or cream cardstock

stamp | RUBBERMOON WRAPPED GIFT DESIGN |

solvent or dye ink pad (black)

chalk (several colors)

cotton swabs

rubber brushes

eraser

craft knife

Another Fun Technique

COTTON SWABS MAKE GREAT CHALK APPLICATORS. Some stamping supplies can be found around your own home. Cotton swabs, for example, make excellent tools for applying chalk over a stamped design. As before, use rubber brushes to blend the chalk.

1 With a craft knife, scrape piles of different colored chalk onto a scrap piece of paper. Pick up the chalk with a cotton swab, then add it to the stamped design.

2 Touch up any mistakes with an eraser.

3 Use a rubber brush to blend the chalk and add any finishing touches to the design.

Materials

colored (greenish-yellow) cardstock

colored (olive), patterned vellum, 8½" x 11" (22cm x 28cm) sheet

background stamp and solid image stamp
| JUDIKINS CIRCLE PATTERN DESIGN; JUDIKINS PURSE DESIGN |

light-colored pigment ink pad (white)

dye ink pad (green)

ruler

craft knife

glue stick

sticker or envelope sealer (optional)

tip Shadow stamping always looks better when the solid stamp is cleaned well before the first inking. Silicone remains on rubber after it has been vulcanized, making the surface resistant to inks and difficult to print from. Using a good solvent cleaner prior to stamping is a must to remove the silicone.

Shadow Stamping

The technique of shadow stamping has been around since the beginning of rubber stamps. These flat, positive surface stamps had been called everything from "palette stamps" to "reversing blocks" until the all-encompassing term of "shadow stamps" finally came to be. The effect of shadow stamping is created by layering one simple stamp design on top of another, allowing you to create many different looks for one single stamp image. Color and ink type are important factors in this technique, as they can make or break the look of the overlapping designs. Begin the project by choosing light-colored pigment ink for the shadow image and a darker colored dye ink for the top image. You can also get marvelous results on dark paper—look at the card pictured on page 36, lower right, for inspiration. If you'd like to try shadow stamping on dark paper, use chalk pigment inks to create a great look.

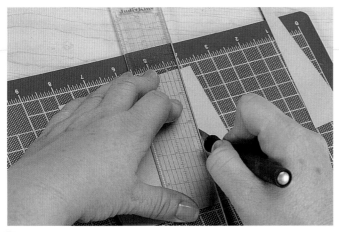

1 Fold the cardstock to create a card, A2 size or smaller. Cut the right edge of the card at an angle, as shown.

2 Ink the background stamp, or "shadow image," with white pigment ink and press onto the front of the card.

3 Ink the image stamp using a dye ink pad. Stamp it directly on top of the stamped background design.

4 To make an envelope, lay the sheet of vellum horizontally on your work surface, then place the card in the center. Fold one-third of the vellum over the card to make a flap. Fold the other third over the flap.

5 Remove the card from the center and completely unfold the vellum. Score the sides to fit the card, leaving an extra 1/16" (2mm) on each side, which will allow the card to slide in and out of the envelope easily. Trim along the scored lines of the top two panels. Leave the bottom panel with the scored flaps attached.

6 Fold in the flaps of the bottom panel, then bring the panel up to meet the middle panel. Adhere the flaps with a glue stick. Place the card in the envelope. To seal, use a sticker, glue stick or envelope sealer.

Materials

papier-mâché box

stamp | JUDIKINS FLOURISH DESIGN |

white pigment ink pad

white acrylic paint or gesso

embossing powder (pastel color)

paintbrush

heat gun

Embossing on Papier-Mâché

There are so many papier-mâché products that can be easily stamped. Boxes, ornaments and picture frames are just a few of the papier-mâché objects I like to keep on hand. In a pinch, I can stamp them and use them for quick gifts. Or, I can emboss papier-mâché boxes with a single image as a wonderful, heartfelt way to present a gift. In this project, I began by priming the papier-mâché surface with white acrylic paint, which makes the light tones of the stamping design stand out.

tips For better coverage, add a layer of ink onto the stamp, then let the ink set. Re-ink the stamp, then press onto the surface.

A papier-mâché surface is quick to soak up ink, so be sure that the ink pad is very wet when you're stamping on papier-mâché.

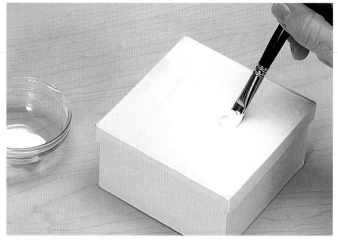

1 Coat the box and the lid with white acrylic paint or a thin layer of gesso. Allow the paint to dry.

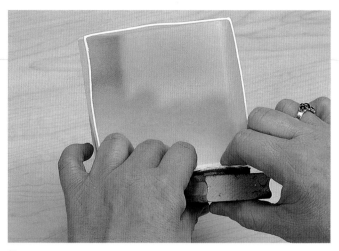

2 Ink the stamp with white pigment ink and stamp the design around the box (see *Tips*, page 46). Stamp off the edges of the box for a more complete and more professional appearance.

3 While the ink is still wet, pour pastel embossing powder over the stamped designs. Continue stamping and adding embossing powder on all sides of the box. Set the embossing powder with a heat gun, holding the gun ½"–1" (13mm–3cm) away from the paper surface.

4 Stamp the lid with the same design using white pigment ink, then pour more of the pastel embossing powder over the stamped surface.

5 Set the embossing powder on the lid with a heat gun.

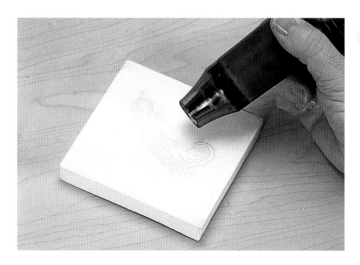

precut pyramid box (available at any scrapbook
store that has a die cut machine)

artist carving block | MASTERCARVE BY STAEDTLER |

scrap paper

dye or pigment ink pad (any color)

pigment ink pad (metallic silver)

black tassel

pencil

craft knife

linoleum cutter

double-sided tape

heat gun

hole punch or Japanese screw punch

Carving Your Own Stamps

You don't have to be a stamping expert to custom make your own
stamp design. In fact, carving your own stamps is quite easy, especially if you begin with simple shapes. For this project, I chose two
familiar designs that are not too complex—a star and a spiral. Once
you become comfortable with the carving technique, you can move
on to more detailed, more imaginative designs. You may find creating your own stamps to be an addiction all its own!

tip Technically a bookbinder's
instrument, the Japanese
screw punch can be found in
many papercrafters' kits. The screw
punch is a great tool because it can
be placed and used anywhere on a
surface, even in the very center.
A regular hole punch, on the other
hand, is limited by how far it can
reach. With the screw punch, you
can make holes of various sizes
in any paper, leather, clay or even
thin metal surface. This tool will
punch through many layers at a time,
which is why bookbinders love it.
When using a Japanese screw
punch, place your thumb on the top
of the tool and press straight up and
down on the surface.

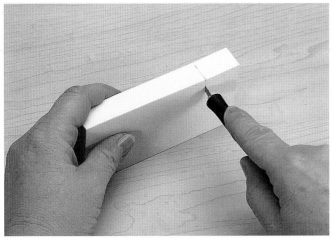

1 Using a craft knife, cut the carving block to the size you'd like your stamp to be.

2 Draw a simple star design on the block with a pencil.

3 Cut along each pencil line with the craft knife, penetrating about ¼" (6mm) through the carving block. Try to keep all the cuts at a 90° angle to the block. Even the slightest deviation in angle will create a bevel under the design, which can cause stamping instability.

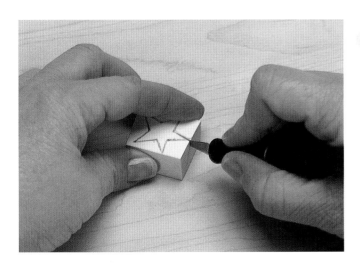

4 Remove the area around the star shape by carefully slicing the knife blade ¼" (6mm) deep into the block, parallel to the top surface. Cut to the perimeter lines of the star, but do not overcut or you risk removing the positive part of the stamp.

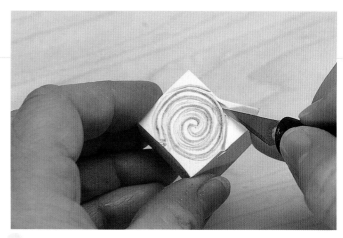

5 Cut another piece of carving block to a similar size. With a pencil, draw a simple swirl design on top of the block. Use a linoleum cutter to carve out the interior openings within the swirl shape.

6 Remove the four corner edges around the swirl, cutting about ¼" (6mm) deep as you did in step 4.

7 Test your stamps on scrap paper using either dye or pigment ink.

8 Using pigment ink, stamp some stars onto the exterior of the unfolded precut pyramid box. Run the stamps off the edge and vary the direction to give the pattern a random appearance.

9 Stamp some swirls onto the unfolded box surface with the same pigment ink, maintaining the random look by stamping off the edge of the box and varying the orientation of the design.

10 Allow the ink to dry. Because it can take a while for pigment ink to dry, you can set the ink with a heat gun to save time.

11 Apply double-sided tape along the side tabs of the box. (You can also use glue, but it will not hold as well as double-sided tape.) Use the craft knife to peel up the top layer of the tape, exposing the adhesive.

12 Construct the box, folding it and pressing the sides against the double-sided tape.

13 Punch a hole in the center of the lid. Attach and secure the tassel through the hole. Fold down the side flaps of the lid, then place the lid on top of the box.

Materials

colored, printed cardstock | ANNA GRIFFIN PURPLE FLOURISH DESIGN |

template stamp and ornamental stamp | ALIAS SMITH AND ROWE BOOKMARK TEMPLATE; JUDIKINS FLOURISH DESIGN |

ink pad (any kind and color)

clear embossing ink pad or light-colored pigment ink pad | VERSAMARK WATERMARK STAMP PAD |

white powdered pigment | PEARL EX |

small, stiff brush

craft knife

matte spray fixative or aerosol hair spray

tip Pearl Ex powdered pigment will adhere to any damp surface. To make it permanent, however, you must apply a spray fixative or a light coat of aerosol hair spray. You can also use a product like Perfect Pearls, which contains gum arabic mixed with raw pigment powder. Gum arabic will keep the powder fixed to the paper.

Overstamping with Powdered Pigments

I always keep plenty of powdered pigments in my stash of stamping supplies, and my favorite brand is Pearl Ex. These pigments can be combined with many kinds of inks, adhesives and paints to create a pearlized metallic effect. This bookmark requires only a single color, white Pearl Ex, but the results are fantastic. You can embellish the finished bookmark by tying on decorative tassels or ribbons. Or, personalize it with metal alphabet stickers, which are widely available at scrapbook stores.

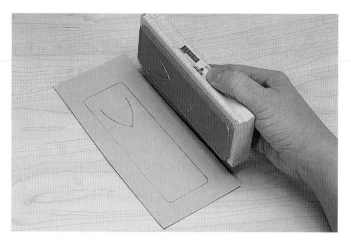

1 Using any ink, stamp on the back side of the printed cardstock with the bookmark pattern stamp.

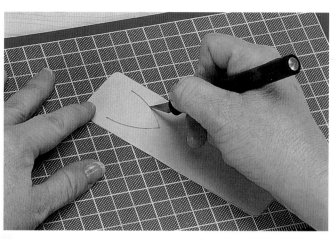

2 Use a craft knife to cut out the bookmark. Create a V-slot by cutting along the "V" lines stamped on the paper.

3 Ink the ornamental stamp with clear embossing ink or light-colored pigment ink. Randomly stamp the front of the bookmark over the printed design. Make sure the ink is very wet.

4 Quickly pour the powdered pigment over the wet ink. Let it sit for a few seconds.

5 Dust off the powder using a small, stiff brush.

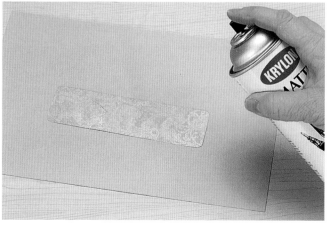

6 Fix the powder by applying matte spray fixative or aerosol hair spray over the front of the bookmark.

Materials ● ● ●

colored (ochre) cardstock with matte finish

mica

template stamp and image stamps | RUBBERMOON
SMALL BOX TEMPLATE; RUBBERMOON PERCHED BIRD
FRAME DESIGN; RUBBERMOON CHILD IN SNOWSTORM
IMAGE DESIGN |, *see Tips, below*

black pigment ink pad

colored pencils (several colors)

glitter

ruler

craft knife

scissors

glue stick or double-sided tape

heat gun (optional)

Using Colored Pencil to Color Stamped Images

Colored pencils are a fabulous way to add color to stamped and embossed images. Easy to find and easy to use, they are ideal for stampers of all levels. Treat yourself to a set of high-quality artist's pencils. You will immediately notice the difference between your pencils and the student-grade colored pencils you may remember from your school days. The better the pencils, the less time and effort you'll spend trying to get the tones and colors you desire.

tips

For this project, you can use any kind of stamp that includes a frame in the image.

When using a template stamp, remember that dotted lines are scored and solid lines are cut.

Electric sharpeners are great—but not for sharpening colored pencils. I prefer to sharpen my colored pencils to a chisel tip using a craft knife or a good handheld sharpener. These tools seem to cause less breakage.

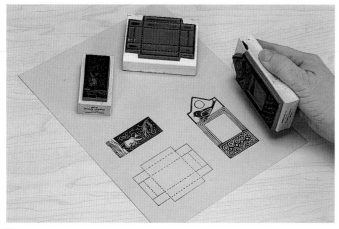

1 Ink the stamps with black pigment ink, then press each onto the same sheet of cardstock. You can use a heat gun to set the ink quickly. Cut each stamped image out.

2 Score the dotted lines of the template stamp. For a crisp line, use the back side of a craft knife tip.

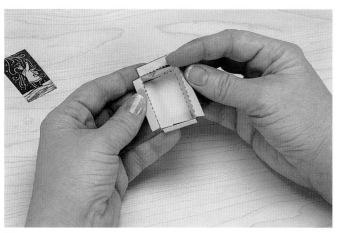

3 Fold the box along the scored lines.

tip When working in colored pencil on a medium- to dark-colored background paper, prime the surface in white pencil first. This will intensify the result of the colored pencil you add, brightening the color and making it "pop." This base will also aid in the blending of colors.

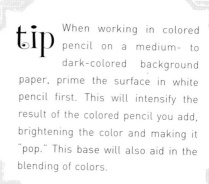

4 Cut out the interior opening of the frame stamp. Prime the uninked areas of the stamped frame and stamped image with white colored pencil (see *Tip*, above).

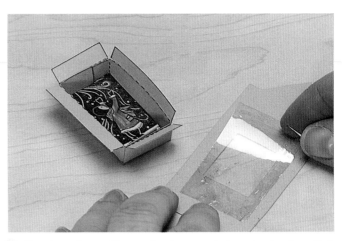

5 Color the frame and the image with colored pencil, blending as desired. Avoid covering any of the stamped lines since the colored pencil will give the inked areas a chalky appearance.

6 Cut the mica to fit over the frame window. Apply glue stick or double-sided tape around the edges on the back of the frame and adhere the mica.

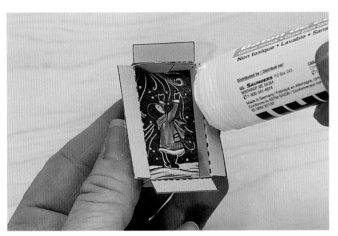

7 Apply glue stick or double-sided tape to the top flaps of the box.

8 Add some glitter inside the box.

9 Secure the glitter inside by adhering the frame to the top flaps of the box.

Materials

dark-colored (black) uncoated cardstock

white cardstock

template stamp and image stamps | RUBBERMOON SMALL BOX TEMPLATE; RUBBERMOON SUNBURST FRAME DESIGN; POSTMODERN PRAYING HANDS DESIGN |

black pigment ink pad

black embossing powder

bleach

colored pencils (several colors)

synthetic-bristle paintbrush or water brush

water spritzer

craft knife or scissors

double-sided tape

heat gun

Another Fun Technique

YOU CAN PRIME A SURFACE WITH BLEACH. When working on very dark paper, bleach can be used to lighten the surface for colored pencil. Bleach adds terrific dimension to a tiny piece like this little shrine.

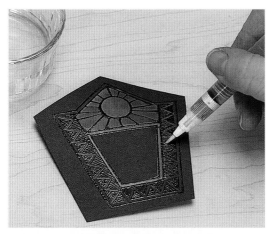

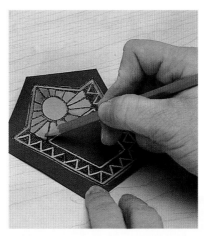

1 Using pigment ink, stamp the frame design and the box template on the dark uncoated cardstock. Pour embossing powder over the ink on the frame, then remove the excess powder. Use the heat gun to set the embossing powder. With a paintbrush or water brush, add bleach in between the embossed areas. To stop the action of the bleach, spritz the area with water. Be sure to rinse your brush very well after using the bleach.

2 When the bleach is dry, add colored pencil over the bleached areas. If you make a mistake, spritz the area with water and wipe with a paper towel. Let the paper dry or apply a heat gun for a few seconds, then recolor.

3 Cut along the solid lines and score the dotted lines of the template to assemble the box. Stamp the image onto white cardstock and add color with colored pencils. Cut the image out and adhere it to the interior of the box, placing it where the frame opening will be. Adhere the frame to the top flaps of the box with double-sided tape.

Materials

small wooden box with lid

stamp | HERO ARTS BLOCK DESIGN |

solvent ink pad (black)

felt-tip marker (black)

colored pencils (several colors)

gloss spray varnish

tip Re-ink your pads before starting a project on wood. Wood is very porous and will absorb a great deal of ink.

Using Colored Pencil on Wood

You've used colored pencil with stamps on paper—now, for a unique look, try using colored pencil on wood. On a soft wood like this pine box, the resulting color is saturated and easy to blend. There are several ready-made wood products that are perfect for stamping projects—picture frames, boxes, ornaments, trays and loads of household items. Look for unfinished wood pieces, which are the easiest to stamp with solvent or even pigment ink. For this technique, I recommend using solvent ink because it dries quickly and holds up well on wood. You can also use pigment ink, but it takes longer to dry.

1 Ink the stamp using solvent ink. Stamp the sides of the wooden box. As you stamp, line up the edges to make one continuous design, but vary the pattern by alternately shifting the stamp up or down. Stamp the top of the lid.
Note: The curved sides of this lid are too grainy, so a stamped image would appear mottled and unclear. For this reason, I positioned the stamp to create a pattern on the top of the lid only.

2 If necessary, use a felt-tip marker to touch up the stamped design.

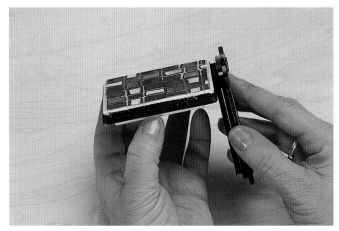

3 Use colored pencils to add color to the box and the top of the lid. Basecoating the areas first with white pencil will make the colors appear brighter.

4 Ink the sides of the lid by rubbing the surface of the ink pad along each edge. If necessary, touch up the sides of the lid with a felt-tip marker.

5 Spray the box and the lid with gloss varnish.

Materials

metal sheet | ART EMBOSS SILVER |

spiral-bound blank book with medium to heavyweight cardboard cover

stamp with interior opening | RUBBERMOON CIRCLE DESIGN WITH ROSETTES |

pigment ink pad (black)

dye ink pad (black), optional

embossing powder (black)

felt-tip markers (several colors)

metal foil tape (silver), 1/2" (13mm) wide, *see Tip, below*

small paintbrush

pencil

eraser

craft knife

scissors

double-sided tape

heat gun

Embossing on Metal

Metal provides a beautiful surface for stamping and is easily enhanced with the addition of embossing powder. Hot metal tends to pick up stray bits of powder, which sometimes makes this technique a challenge for first-time embossers. For this reason, I recommend practicing on paper several times before trying the metal. Be sure that the metal sheet is nice and cool before starting the project. An easy way to prepare the metal is to stick it in the refrigerator for a few minutes before beginning.

tip Brass, copper and silver foil tape can be found at most stained glass supply shops. Most foil tape is available in several different widths.

1 Use pigment ink to stamp a design onto a flattened sheet of metal (see *Tip*, below). Pour embossing powder over the stamped design, then brush off the excess powder with a small paintbrush.

2 Heat the embossing powder, holding the heat gun about 1/2"–1" (13mm–3cm) away from the surface of the metal sheet. When finished, use a felt-tip marker for touch-ups if necessary. Add color to the stamped design with felt-tip markers.

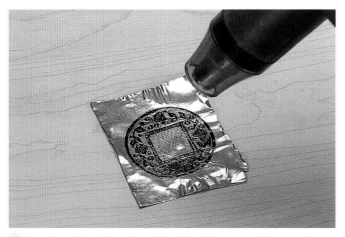

tip For the best results, the metal sheet should be as flat as possible before stamping on it. If necessary, flatten the metal by running a ruler across the back of the sheet.

3 Set the colored marker ink with a heat gun. Cut out the design, trimming along the perimeter with scissors.

4 Use a craft knife to cut out the center window from the stamped design. Position the stamped metal piece on the book cover, placing it at the center. Hold the piece in place with one hand, then use a pencil to trace the inside perimeter of the window onto the cover.

5 With a craft knife, cut just outside the pencil lines to create a window on the book cover.

6 Place the stamped metal design on the cover so that the two window openings line up, then secure the metal piece to the cover with double-sided tape. For a decorative touch, apply two strips of metal tape to the cover, one on either side of the center piece, as shown.

7 With the book closed, use a pencil to trace along the inside of the window, marking the first blank page underneath the cover. Using either pigment ink or dye ink, stamp an image within the penciled lines to appear through the window. When the ink is dry, erase the pencil marks.

tips If the edges of the window opening on the book cover look rough, use an emery board to smooth them out.

Permanent felt-tip markers now come in so many colors that you can even touch up gold and silver embossing powder colors!

Materials

scraps of metal sheet |ART EMBOSS COPPER|

cardstock (patterned)

stamp |RUBBERMOON MOON FACE DESIGN |

pigment ink pad (black)

embossing powder (copper)

scissors

double-sided tape

heat gun

Another Fun Technique

TURN SCRAP METAL PIECES INTO EMBELLISHMENTS. You can make tiny card embellishments with those leftover metal sheet pieces. Choose embossing powder that matches the metal surface, then emboss the stamped design. Here I used a copper-on-copper color combination. Silver-on-silver would be perfect for an elegant wedding or anniversary card!

1 Flatten the scrap piece of metal by running the edge of a ruler across the surface.

2 Stamp a design onto the metal surface using pigment ink. Pour embossing powder over the stamped design and brush off the excess powder, then set with a heat gun.

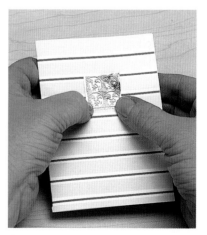

3 Trim the stamped design with scissors. Attach the metal piece to the front of a card with double-sided tape.

two sheets of cardstock (light blue striped)

background stamp, solid image stamp and template stamp | HERO ARTS GRID AND DOTS DESIGN; JUDIKINS HEART DESIGN; ALIAS SMITH AND ROWE PURSE TEMPLATE |

chalk pigment ink pads, two colors (gray and light green)

craft knife

scissors

double-sided tape

heat gun

Overstamping

These days, it seems that crafters have a million different patterned paper designs at their fingertips. You can give printed paper a more customized look by stamping over the pattern. For successful overstamping results, keep the combination of design elements simple and always use a lighter-colored ink for the bottom stamp. Select paper with a basic pattern, such as stripes or polka dots, and choose stamps with basic graphic images. With the purse template stamp that I use in this project, you can make impressive little shower favors!

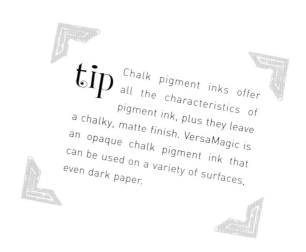

tip Chalk pigment inks offer all the characteristics of pigment ink, plus they leave a chalky, matte finish. VersaMagic is an opaque chalk pigment ink that can be used on a variety of surfaces, even dark paper.

1 Using the lighter-colored chalk pigment ink, stamp the background design onto the sheet of cardstock. Repeat with another sheet of the same cardstock.

2 Ink the solid image stamp with the darker-colored chalk pigment ink, then stamp directly over the background design on the two sheets of cardstock. Set the ink with a heat gun. Once the ink has dried, it will have a matte, chalky appearance.

3 Turn the sheets of cardstock over. Ink the template stamp with either color of chalk pigment ink and stamp onto the back of each sheet. Cut along the solid lines with scissors and score along the dotted lines with the back of a craft knife tip.

4 Make sure that all of the ink is dry. Attach the two pieces to construct a three-dimensional purse, using double-sided tape to secure it. (The double-sided tape will not adhere to wet ink.)

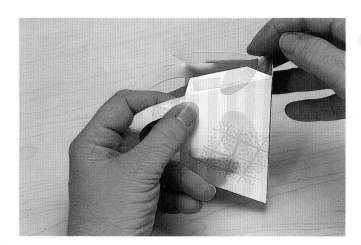

5 Fold in the side flaps to complete the purse, then secure the flaps in place with double-sided tape.

Materials

white coated matte cardstock | JUDIKINS MATTEKOTE |

white cardstock, coated or uncoated

stamps | JUDIKINS ABSTRACT OVALS DESIGN; JUDIKINS
ATOMIC DESIGN; JUDIKINS CAT DESIGN |

clear embossing ink pad | VERSAMARK WATERMARK
STAMP PAD |

light-colored and dark-colored dye ink pads
(pink and violet)

black dye ink pad

black felt-tip marker (optional)

silver colored pencil

brayer

ruler

craft knife

double-sided tape

Using Resist

Using resist is a fundamental technique that every stamper should know. This technique is based on the concept that most types of ink resist each other. Working from this concept, you can generate all kinds of interesting effects. A great look for retro stamps can be created by stamping a pattern onto paper with clear embossing ink, then using a brayer to apply dye ink on top. The clear ink resists the color ink, leaving a paler pattern underneath. Paper is an important factor in resists, as the ink needs to set quickly. I recommend JudiKins MatteKote, which features a clay-coated finish that is not shiny but holds color well. Resists will work on shiny coated papers, but the stamped imagery will not be as crisp.

tip Useful for more than just applying ink to paper, a good soft rubber brayer is a handy tool for papercrafting. A brayer is great for sealing layers of paper together and for inking large stamps evenly.

1 Use a clear embossing ink pad to randomly stamp an image a few times onto a sheet of coated matte cardstock. With the same ink, stamp another image onto the cardstock, occasionally overlapping the existing stamps.

2 Ink the brayer by pressing the individual ink pads against the surface of the roller, covering it with ink. Apply the light-colored dye ink first, followed by the dark color. You can also use a rainbow ink pad for a multicolor effect.

3 Make sure the clear ink has dried on the cardstock, then ink the sheet by rolling the brayer across it.

4 When the ink has dried, trim the cardstock so it is a little less than half the size of the overall sheet.

5 Using black dye ink, stamp the cat image onto the lower left corner of the inked cardstock. If necessary, touch up the image with a black felt-tip marker.

6 Accent the cat's eyes with a silver colored pencil, lightening and evening the color of the eyes as necessary.

7 Edge the cardstock with the darker-colored ink pad.

8 Fold a sheet of white cardstock in half to make a card. Attach the stamped cardstock to the front of the card using double-sided tape.

Materials

white coated matte cardstock | JUDIKINS MATTEKOTE |

stamps | RUBBERMOON SILHOUETTED WOMAN DESIGNS |

pigment ink pad (black)

dye ink pad (green)

brayer

Another Fun Technique

PIGMENT INKS MAKE GREAT RESISTS, TOO. When dry, pigment ink will resist other inks just like clear embossing ink will. When selecting your inks, choose colors that work well together.

1 Use pigment ink to stamp a design on coated matte cardstock. Ink the brayer with dye ink, then roll it across the cardstock to create a background.

Materials

white coated matte cardstock | JUDIKINS MATTEKOTE |
stamp | RUBBERMOON BAMBOO BRANCH DESIGN |
light-colored chalk pigment ink pad (light green)
dark-colored dye ink pad (magenta)
brayer

Another Fun Technique

WHEN USED AS A RESIST, LIGHT-COLORED PIGMENT INK WILL LEAVE A SOFT SHADE OF COLOR BEHIND. You can cover the light resist with a darker dye ink for beautiful, subtle results. This can be a convenient solution when you wish to cover a large area with color or want to use up old or stained paper.

1 Stamp a design onto a sheet of coated matte cardstock using light-colored chalk pigment ink.

2 Ink the brayer with darker dye ink, then roll the brayer across the cardstock to create a background color.

Materials

white coated matte cardstock | JUDIKINS
MATTEKOTE |

large paper tag, 5½" x 5½" (14cm x 14cm)

solid image stamp and ornamental stamp
| JUDIKINS HEART DESIGN; JUDIKINS SCROLLING
VINE DESIGN |

dye ink pads (green and pink)

scissors

double-sided tape

Stamping on a Rubber Stamp

You can enrich your stamp collection by broadening the number of stamping effects you are able to achieve
with just a few different stamps. This technique combines two stamp designs for a brand new look. By using
intricately detailed stamps over solid positive surface stamps, the possibilities for creating new images are
limitless. Look for solid images or geometric patterns that could be used in many ways as well as images
that have personal meaning to you.

tips For this technique, it is
important that the orna-
mental stamp be clean
and dry between stampings. This will
allow the surface to pick up excess
ink from the solid image stamp.

If a card measures under 3½" (9cm) or
over 5" (13cm) square, it will require
extra postage.

1 Ink the solid image stamp with dye ink, then press the stamp onto a sheet of coated matte cardstock.

2 Re-ink the stamp with the same color. Make sure that the ornamental stamp is clean and dry, then press it onto the wet ink of the solid stamp. Pull off the ornamental stamp to leave a design on the solid stamp. Stamp the image onto the cardstock, next to the first stamp. Clean the ornamental design stamp and allow it to dry completely.

3 Wipe off the solid stamp, re-ink it with a different color, then stamp it onto the cardstock. Re-ink the solid stamp again and repeat step 2 to create the fourth and final stamp on the cardstock.

4 Ink the ornamental stamp with one of the two dye ink colors previously used, then stamp a decorative background onto one side of the paper tag. Run the dye pad along each edge of the tag for a final touch.

5 Cut the four stamped images into separate squares. Use double-sided tape to attach them to the stamped side of the tag in a square arrangement.

Materials

papier-mâché ornament

main image stamp and background pattern
stamp | RUBBERMOON BIRTHDAY CAKE DESIGN;
SMALL HANDMADE STAR DESIGN |

solvent ink pad (black)

pigment ink pad (white)

dimensional glue | DIAMOND GLAZE |

water-soluble crayons or watercolor paints
(several colors)

glitter

water brush or paintbrush

tip This ornament is hollow, which makes it difficult to apply even pressure as you are stamping the surface. When working with this kind of surface, I choose stamps with smaller images.

Creating Watercolor Effects

Water-soluble crayons can be used in so many ways, you'll find yourself using them all the time. In fact, just one set of these crayons does the job of several other supplies. In this project, the crayons are used in place of watercolor paints. Water-soluble crayons give the richest color of any medium. They can be applied directly on rubber stamps, paper, wood and much more, and they can be used wet or dry. Here, I use water-soluble crayons on a brown papier-mâché ornament that could be added to a gift box as a tag or embellishment.

1 Ink the main image stamp with solvent ink, then press the stamp onto the front center of the papier-mâché ornament.

2 Color in the stamped image and part of the background with water-soluble crayons or watercolor paints.

3 Blend the color with a little water, using a water brush or a paintbrush.

4 Color the edges of the ornament with water-soluble crayons or watercolor paints. If using crayons, blend the color with a water brush or paintbrush.

5 Using a small and simple stamp, stamp a background design around the main image with pigment ink.

6 Randomly squeeze small dots of dimensional glue between the background stamps.

7 Sprinkle glitter onto the ornament, then gently tap to remove excess glitter. Allow the glue to set.

Materials

1¹/₄" x 1" (3cm x 2.5cm) presanded glass rune tiles | APPALOOSA ART | or mosaic glass pieces

bracelet with flat, square links ("no. 7 bracelet" in many jewelry supply catalogs)

stamp | RUBBERMOON BAMBOO BRANCH DESIGN |

pigment ink pad (gray)

embossing powder (copper)

dimensional glue | DIAMOND GLAZE |

epoxy glue | UHU CREATIV´ |

glass cutter

heat gun or oven

sandpaper, if using mosaic pieces

tip If you are embossing a lot of tiles, place them in an oven to emboss. Bake the tiles at 400°F (204°C) until the embossing powder is fully cooked (see page 23 for further detail).

Stamping on Glass

Like metal, glass takes heat very well, making it an ideal surface for embossing. This technique of embossing on glass allows you to make your own original stamped jewelry. With presanded glass pieces, it's a snap—all you have to do is stamp, emboss and glue the tiles to the bracelet. For this particular bracelet, I cut the glass tiles in half with a basic glass cutter. If you'd rather not cut glass yourself, check out the mosaic section at your local craft store for similar pieces. Most mosaic glass pieces will require a bit of sanding to remove the sharp edges.

1 Cut six or more glass tiles in half. You will need at least eleven halves for a standard no. 7 bracelet (shown above). If you are using a different size bracelet, cut a half tile for each link. Sand the edges of the cut glass if necessary.

2 Use pigment ink to stamp a design onto each tile. If the stamp sticks to the glass, hit the side of the stamp. The glass should release from the stamp.

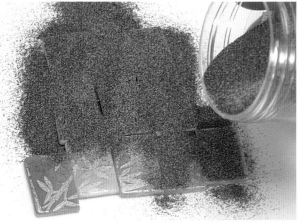

3 Pour embossing powder over the stamped tiles. Shake the excess powder off of each tile.

4 Emboss the tiles with a heat gun or in an oven (see *Tip*, page 74), then let them cool completely.

5 When the tiles are cool, brush dimensional glue over the top of each tile. Allow the glue to dry.

6 Brush epoxy glue onto the metal squares between each bracelet link. Press a tile on top of each square. Work quickly because the epoxy glue dries fast.

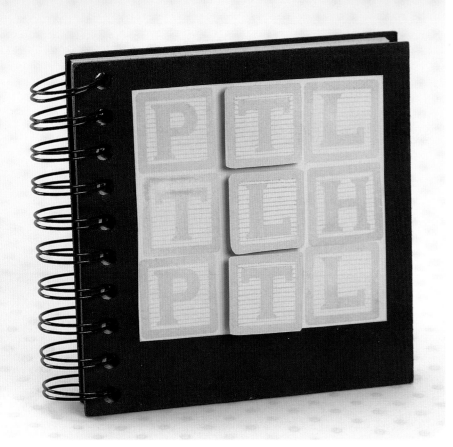

Materials

spiral-bound blank book with medium to heavyweight cardboard cover

light colored (pale yellow) cardstock

balsa wood pieces, approximately ½"–¾" (12mm–19mm) thick, for mounting stamps

unmounted alphabet sheets | POST SCRIPT STUDIO BLOCK ALPHABET LETTERS |

chalk pigment ink pads (gray and light green)

self adhesive foam mounts | 3-D POP DOTS |

scissors

double-sided tape

Working with Unmounted Stamps

When you purchase an unmounted stamp, you are buying just the rubber die without any cushion or wood backing. Many alphabet sets come unmounted in sheets since they can be quite pricey when individually mounted on wood. This technique is a quick and inexpensive way to use unmounted alphabets or other stamps. Instead of a balsa wood block, you can also mount your stamps on acrylic blocks, a popular method of mounting since the transparency of these blocks makes it easy to line up images.

tips Most unmounted rubber stamps are thick enough that no cushion is needed between the mount and the rubber.

If you are spelling a word or phrase, remember it needs to be placed on the mount backwards so it will stamp in the correct sequence.

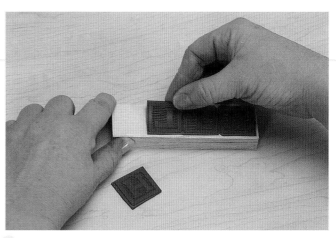

1 Cut out the individual letter stamps with scissors. The blades should cut the rubber at a 90° angle to the sheet to avoid creating a beveled edge.

2 Place a piece of double-sided tape onto one side of the balsa wood block. Remove the top strip from the tape to expose the adhesive. Choose which letters you'd like to include on the stamp, then place the rubber letter stamps on the tape, lining them up edge to edge (see *Tips,* page 76).

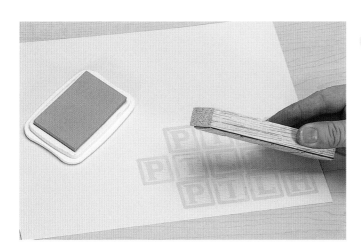

3 Ink the stamp with pigment ink. Press the stamp onto a sheet of cardstock to create several vertical rows of letters. If desired, stamp a few more rows in a different color. Cut out three rows of stamps as well as three individual stamps.

4 Attach the three rows of stamped letters to the cover of the blank book using double-sided tape. Add dimension to the design by adhering a few letters to the cover with foam mounts or a thin piece of balsa wood.

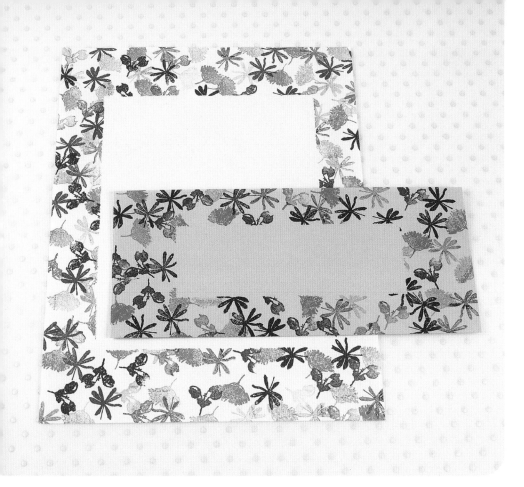

Materials

text weight or stationery paper (white),
8½" x 11" (22cm x 28cm)

envelope (gray), optional

small stamps | HERO ARTS LEAF AND
FLOWER DESIGNS |

ink pads (any kind; green, burgundy
and violet)

ruler

craft knife

art masking tape, 6" (15cm) wide

Creating Borders

Every beginning stamper should learn to master the art of creating borders. You'll
never run out of uses for stamped borders. They can be used on greeting cards,
envelopes, boxes, stationery, scrapbook pages and so much more. Eclipse art masking
tape is perfect for this technique because it can mask an area up to 6" (15cm) wide, plus
it is reusable.

tip Lining up any type of tape
can be a challenge, especially
when you are tense. Pulling
tape tightly before positioning it can
cause a bubble effect. Try to relax the
tape by letting it hang in a natural
curve, then place the bottom of the
curve on the paper first. Allow the
remaining tape to fall gently into place.

1 With a craft knife, cut a 8½" x 6" (22cm x 15cm) piece of art masking tape.

2 Position the tape in the center of the paper.

3 Using your choice of stamps and inks, stamp the exposed paper. Be sure to stamp off the edges of the paper and the tape, especially in the corner areas. Vary the orientation of the stamps for a random pattern.

4 Remove the tape.

5 To create a border on one side of an envelope, position the same piece of tape across the front of the envelope 1½" (4cm) from the left edge. Stamp the area to the left of the tape, remembering to stamp off the edge of the envelope and vary the direction of the stamp. Remove the tape.

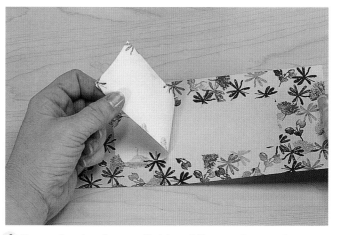

6 To create a border on all sides of the envelope, cut a 6" x 2" (15cm x 5cm) strip of art masking tape. Position it across the front center of the envelope. Stamp around the tape, remembering to stamp off the edges and vary the direction of the stamp. Remove the tape.

terra-cotta flowerpot

white tissue paper

stamp | RUBBERMOON TREE BRANCH DESIGN |

dye ink pads (blue, yellow and red)

paintbrush

dimensional glue | DIAMOND GLAZE |

tip Stamping on unglazed pottery is fun, and it works well with any outdoor craft paint. Choose smaller stamps for stamping directly onto the pot. Always roll the stamp across the curved surface of the pot in one continuous motion. Larger stamps work better when they are stamped on tissue and then découpaged onto the pot, as shown in this project. Covering the tissue with a coat of dimensional glue gives the pot a ceramic-like layer and makes it suitable for outdoor use.

Stamping on Tissue Paper

Stamped and personalized, tissue paper makes great gift wrap and bag filler. It is also excellent for découpage since the tissue becomes transparent when dry and can be layered. Stamping on tissue paper can be a bit tricky. Because the paper is so thin, the ink tends to bleed through it. This is why choosing and testing the ink before starting the project is an important preliminary step.

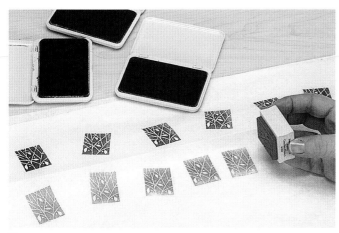

1 Using dye ink, stamp the tissue paper. Make three horizontal rows of the same stamp, each row in a different color.

2 Tear the tissue paper to divide the rows, then tear off the stamps into individual pieces.

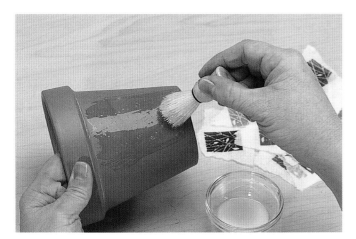

3 Coat the terra-cotta pot with a layer of dimensional glue.

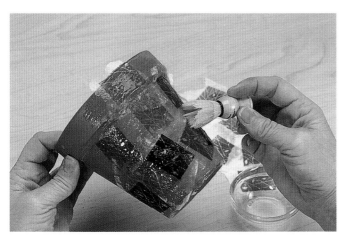

4 Layer the pieces of stamped tissue paper over the coated surface in a random pattern around the entire pot. Brush more glue over the top of the tissue paper pieces to adhere them to the pot.

Materials

Ribbon

ribbon (cream)

image stamp and alphabet stamps | JUDIKINS HEART DESIGN; POSTMODERN LETTERS |

contrasting pigment ink pads (metallic copper and black)

Wrapping Paper

plain wrapping paper (gold)

background stamp and solid image stamp | JUDIKINS DOUBLE HEART DESIGN; JUDIKINS SOLID HEART DESIGN |

pigment ink pad (metallic copper)

dye ink pad (metallic silver)

Gift Card

cardstock (cream, to match ribbon)

solid image stamp | JUDIKINS SOLID HEART DESIGN |

ruler

craft knife

heat gun

hole punch or Japanese screw punch

Creating Gift Wrap

I love making my own gift wrap with stamps, or at least accenting printed wrap with a few stamped images. The key is to create the paper ahead of the need so that you'll be ready to wrap at a moment's notice. When stamped, simple brown or white butcher paper makes marvelous gift wrap. You can also stamp matching ribbons, gift tags and other embellishments to create a gift wrap ensemble. Anybody that receives a gift in this wrapping is sure to be impressed—even before they find out what's inside!

tip Use caution when using heat to set ink on unusual surfaces. For example, if you are stamping on synthetic ribbon, don't heat too harshly. A better option for setting ink on synthetic ribbon is to use a hair dryer.

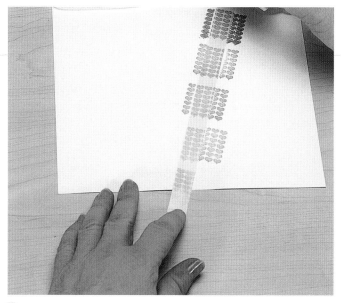

1 Using metallic pigment ink, stamp a design down the length of the ribbon.

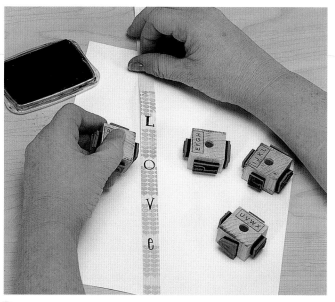

2 Using a contrasting pigment ink, stamp a word or phrase down the length of the ribbon with alphabet stamps.

1 Ink a decorative background stamp with the same pigment ink used for the ribbon design. Then, stamp the design in rows across a sheet of wrapping paper.

2 Ink a solid image stamp with dye ink. Stamp the image over the background design on the wrapping paper, again working in rows.

1 Score and fold the cardstock to create a card. Ink the solid image stamp with the same metallic pigment ink used for the ribbon design and the wrapping paper. Press the stamp onto the front of the card, lining up the left edge of the stamp flush with the fold. Make a few stamps in a vertical row along the edge of the card, as shown.

2 Set the ink with a heat gun.

3 Cut the right edge of the card with a craft knife to make a long, narrow card.

4 Use a craft knife to trim the front of the card, cutting away any negative space around or between the stamps.

5 Using the same metallic pigment ink as before, stamp the inside of the card with the design used for the ribbon.

6 Wrap a package using the stamped paper and an unstamped ribbon and bow. Tie the stamped ribbon to the bow so it is visible on top of the package.

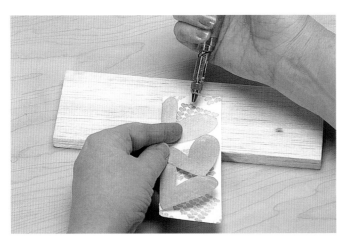

7 Punch a hole at the top of the back flap of the card.

8 Attach the card to the package by tying a piece of ribbon from the bow through the hole of the card.

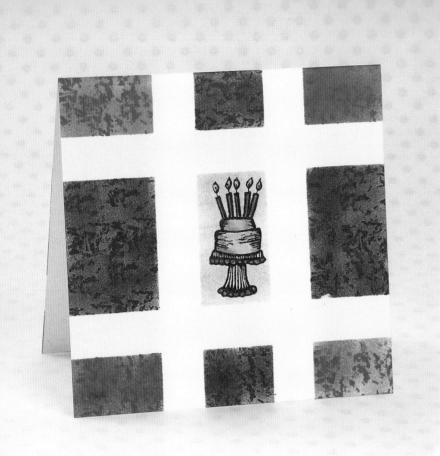

Materials

white cardstock

main image stamp and background pattern stamp | RUBBERMOON BIRTHDAY CAKE DESIGN; JUDIKINS INK BLOT DESIGN |

dye ink pads (orange, red and blue)

colored pencils (several colors)

makeup sponges

art masking tape or drafting tape (use drafting tape if you plan to apply a lot of color)

tip Sponges come in a variety of weights and densities. The density of the sponge affects the application of ink. A denser sponge will apply more color, while an airier sponge will apply less.

Sponging and Color Blocking

Sponges make it easy to apply color to your printing surface. With this quick tape method of color blocking, you can create a brilliant background in no time at all. The technique of color blocking can be customized to work with any size stamp, which makes it ideal for a wide variety of stamp sizes and designs.

1 Apply tape to the cardstock. Cross vertical pieces over horizontal pieces at 90° angles to form a grid. Adjust the size of the openings to accommodate the stamp images that you'll be using. Once in place, press the tape firmly onto the paper so that there is no chance of ink leaking or bleeding.

2 Load sponges with your choice of dye ink, then sponge the ink onto the paper, keeping each color separate and within the masked blocks. The more ink you apply, the more intense the color will be. Apply only a light layer of ink to the central block.

3 Stamp the main image over the central block of sponged color, using dye ink. Keep the image within the masked block of color.

4 Using dye ink, stamp the background pattern onto the remaining color blocks.

5 Color the central stamped image with colored pencils.

6 Carefully remove the tape.

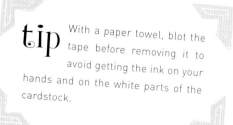

tip With a paper towel, blot the tape before removing it to avoid getting the ink on your hands and on the white parts of the cardstock.

Materials · ● ●

cardboard pillow box

stamp | HERO ARTS SNOWFLAKES DESIGN |

mini pigment ink pads (yellow, red and green)

pigment ink pad (white)

tissue paper (white)

heat gun

small ornament or favor

Inking Directly onto Paper

Another old trick that every stamper should know is how to apply color directly from a stamp pad to the paper. Now that most stamp pads have a raised surface, this technique has become very easy. There are a few helpful hints to remember when inking the paper directly. First, small stamp pads are perfect for this method of coloring. Second, this technique works exceptionally well on uncoated papers and cardboard, like the pillow box used in this project. Finally, when layering ink colors, always work from light to dark.

1 Stamp the lightest-colored mini pigment ink pad directly onto one side of the flattened pillow box. Allow the ink to dry; you'll know it's dry when it loses its shine.

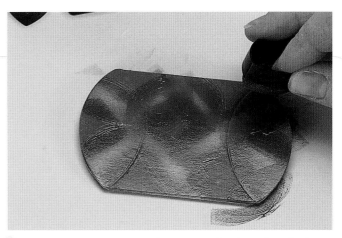

2 Stamp the next mini ink pad directly onto the box, layering this color on top of the first color. Use the shape of the pad to create the pattern. To change the shape of the pattern a bit, twist the pad slightly when stamping to soften the edges of the impression. Allow the ink to dry.

3 Add a third color on top of the second color using the last mini ink pad.

4 Since there is so much ink on the box, use a heat gun to help speed up the drying process. The ink needs to be completely dry before proceeding to the next step.

5 Using pigment ink, stamp a design onto the box.

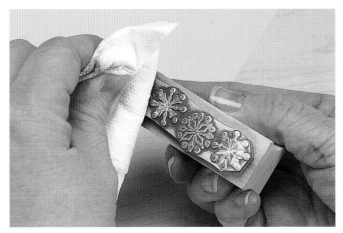

6 In between each stamping, wipe off the stamp to remove the excess color that is picked up from the surface of the box. Re-ink the stamp with the pigment ink, then stamp the surface again.

7 Use the pigment ink to stamp the same design onto a sheet of tissue paper. Allow the ink to dry. Fold the bottom of the pillow box to open it up. Stuff the tissue paper into the box, then insert a small ornament or other fun favor.

Materials ● ● ●

white coated matte cardstock | JUDIKINS MATTEKOTE |

colored (yellow) cardstock, folded into
4¼" x 3½" (11cm x 9cm) card

pattern or texture stamp | JUDIKINS INK BLOT DESIGN |

mini pigment ink pads (yellow, ochre, green
and blue)

pigment ink pad (metallic silver)

ruler

craft knife

art masking tape

double-sided tape (optional)

Another Fun Technique

BE CREATIVE WITH THE PAPER YOU USE FOR CLEANING YOUR STAMP PAD. Don't throw that cardstock away! Recycle it by trimming it down and adding it to the front of a card. There couldn't be an easier way to turn trash into treasure.

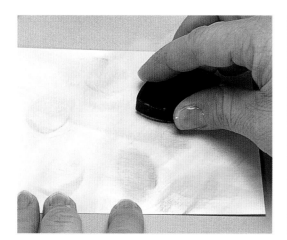

1 Swipe the lightest-colored mini ink pad across the surface of the coated matte cardstock, keeping the swiping motion in the same general direction. Leave some uninked spaces for the next color to show through.

2 Swipe the next mini ink pad across the cardstock, moving the pad in a different direction from step 1. Again allow some areas to remain uninked for the next color to show through.

3 Swipe the next mini ink pad across the cardstock, moving the pad in a different direction from the previous step.

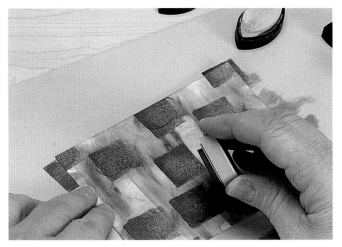

4 Stamp over the inked cardstock with the last mini ink pad, using the shape of the pad to create a pattern.

5 Ink the texture or pattern stamp with pigment ink, then stamp it randomly onto the inked cardstock. Cut the cardstock to 3¾" x 2¾" (10cm x 7cm).

6 Unfold the card and lay it out, exterior side up. On the front of the card, pencil in two 2½" x ¾" (6cm x 19mm) rectangles, each with the top and bottom sides measuring ½" (13mm) from the edge of the paper. Use a craft knife to cut three sides of each rectangle. Leave the top side of each rectangle uncut to make flaps. Place the bottom edge of the ruler flush with the bottom of the card. Cut along the top edge of the ruler to remove part of the flaps. There should be two small flaps remaining.

7 Mask off the front of the card so the two flaps are exposed. Stamp the flaps with the same pattern and the same ink used in step 5.

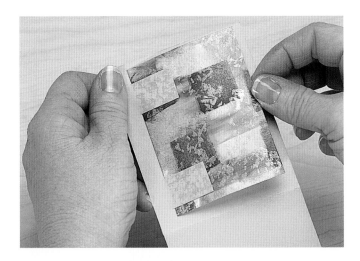

8 Tuck the trimmed, inked cardstock from step 5 into the slots. This card will stay together without adhesive, but you can add double-sided tape for extra security.

Materials

white coated matte cardstock | JUDIKINS MATTEKOTE |

colored (light blue) cardstock

stamp | JUDIKINS TREE DESIGN |

mini pigment ink pads (yellow, light green, dark green and mahogany)

dye ink pads (yellow and blue)

clear embossing powder

makeup sponges

ruler

craft knife

double-sided mounting tape

heat gun

Multicolor Embossing

Stamped designs seem extra fancy when they feature a multicolored image that blends from one tone into another. This effect is easy to achieve with clear embossing powder. For this technique, your stamp image should be a graphic design with a positive surface, which will hold the blended color well. Small ink pads work best for inking the stamp.

1 Ink the right third of a stamp with a light-colored mini pigment ink pad, pressing the pad directly onto the stamp surface. In the same fashion, ink the middle third with a darker-colored mini ink pad and the left third with an even darker mini ink pad. There should be a gradual transition between the three colors. Ink any remaining areas as desired.

2 Press the stamp onto a sheet of coated matte cardstock.

3 Pour clear embossing powder over the stamped surface. Remove the excess powder.

4 Set the embossing powder with a heat gun.

5 Load a sponge with dye ink for your background. Sponge the background color directly onto the paper, right over the stamped image. You can add more than one color, as I did here to represent the sky and the earth.

6 With a craft knife, trim the image to a rectangle that will fit onto the front of an A2 card. Use the darker dye ink pad to edge the stamped cardstock.

7 Score and fold the colored cardstock down the center to make a card. Mount the trimmed image onto the front of the card using double-sided tape.

white cardstock

patterned cardstock (green and red striped)

stamp | HERO ARTS FLOWER DESIGN |

mini pigment ink pad (red)

pigment ink pad (white)

colored (red) embossing powder

thin ribbon (red and white pattern)

scissors

double-sided mounting tape

heat gun

Japanese screw punch or hole punch

Layer Embossing

The technique of layer embossing has been around for a long time. I first tried it by spraying adhesives over the entire surface of a card, resulting in a glassy finish. Since then, many brands have come out with extra thick embossing powders in a wide array of colors. Now, you have the ability to make all kinds of embossed masterpieces with thick, clear powders that are easy to use, like Amazing Glaze.

1 Stamp the mini pigment ink pad several times on the white cardstock to form a square.

2 Pour embossing powder over the inked surface. Emboss the powder with a heat gun.

3 Once the embossing powder is melted, immediately pour on more powder and emboss with a heat gun. Repeat at least three times to get a thick layer of embossed powder.

4 Lightly ink a decorative stamp with pigment ink, then press the stamp onto the embossed layer.

5 Cut a square from the cardstock with scissors, trimming right around the stamped image.

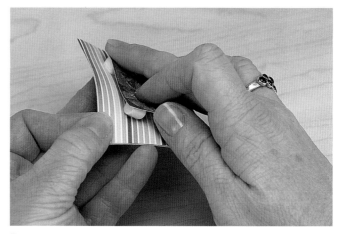

6 Using double-sided mounting tape, adhere the stamped image to the front of a small, folded card made from patterned cardstock.

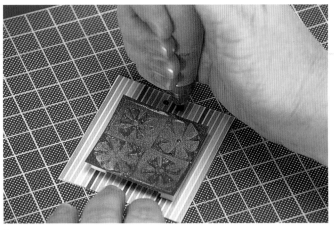 

7 Punch two holes next to each other at the upper center of the card.

8 Thread a piece of ribbon through the two holes, tie a bow and trim the ribbon.

Materials

white cardstock

colored (light blue) cardstock

stamp | RUBBERMOON MOON FACE DESIGN |

pigment ink pads (blue and white)

clear embossing powder

water-soluble crayons (several colors)

ribbon embellishment

craft knife

double-sided tape

heat gun

Another Fun Technique

FAUX ENAMEL EFFECTS ARE EASIER TO ACHIEVE THAN YOU MAY THINK! Once you have mastered layer embossing, try your hand at this technique, which imitates the look of enamel. I recommend using LYRA water-soluble crayons for this technique because they do not break down as quickly in the embossing powder as oil or wax crayons do.

1 Using a brayer or a solid square stamp, ink a sheet of white cardstock with a dense layer of pigment ink. Add a swirling design with a water-soluble crayon. Pour clear embossing powder onto the design, shake off the excess powder and set with a heat gun.

2 Add more detail to the design with a water-soluble crayon in another color. Pour more clear embossing powder onto the design, shake off the excess and set with a heat gun.

3 Repeat step 2, using another color crayon.

4 Thoroughly heat the surface with a heat gun to completely melt the crayon mixture.

5 While the mixture is melted, pull the tip of a craft knife through the surface to swirl the colors, as shown. Trim the design while the mixture is still slightly warm. Once the mixture has set, you can add a stamp design to the surface with pigment ink. Mount the trimmed design to the front of a folded card with double-sided tape. If desired, add a ribbon embellishment along the fold.

tip Adding a bit of white crayon or a drizzle of white embossing powder can brighten a piece that is a bit dark.

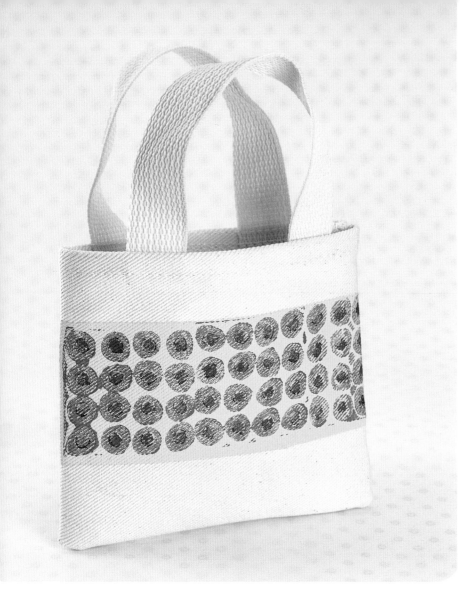

Materials

mini canvas tote bag

stamp | JUDIKINS CIRCLE DESIGN |

lighter- and darker-colored acrylic paint
(yellow and green)

fabric medium, if the item is going to be
washed; if the item is not going to be washed,
fabric medium is not needed

fabric and/or paint markers (several colors),
if the item is going to be washed; if the item
is not going to be washed, felt-tip markers can
be used

small, stiff paintbrush

removable masking tape, *see Tip, below*

tip Art masking tape may not
stick to some fabrics, so use
regular removable masking
tape for this technique.

Stamping on Fabric

With the arrival of new inks, markers, pens and paints on the craft market, stamping
on fabric is now easier than ever. When first trying this technique, start with a simple
surface, such as a fabric scrap or an inexpensive little canvas tote like the one in this
project. Canvas is a great surface for stamping because it will accept paints and inks
beautifully. Explore other fabric surfaces as you feel more comfortable with the
technique. Begin by choosing bold, positive surface images since they work best on all
fabrics. Details can always be added later with markers and pens.

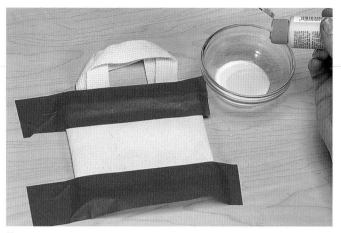

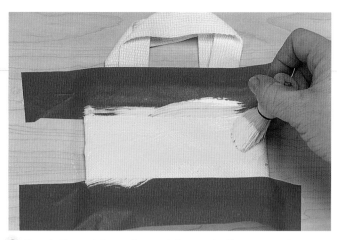

1 Lay the tote bag flat on your work surface. Use removable masking tape to mask off the top and bottom of the bag, leaving a horizontal band of exposed canvas across the front. In a small bowl or container, mix three parts of the lighter-colored acrylic paint to one part fabric medium, or as otherwise instructed on the bottle.

2 Brush the paint-medium mixture onto the exposed canvas surface. Allow the paint to dry.

3 Mix the darker-colored acrylic paint with the fabric medium, as in step 1, then use the mixture to ink the stamp. Press the stamp onto the fabric to create a design across the painted surface. Allow the paint to dry.

4 Color and touch up the stamped design using felt-tip markers. Use fabric markers or paint markers if the item will be washed.

5 Carefully peel off the tape.

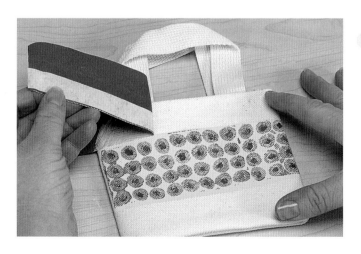

Materials

white cardstock

white A2 card

colored (light blue) A2 card

balsa wood pieces, approximately 1/2"– 3/4" (12mm–19mm) thick, for mounting stamps (if your stamps are unmounted)

main image stamp and background stamp
| POST SCRIPT STUDIO SNOWMAN DESIGN; HERO ARTS SNOWFLAKE DESIGN |

chalk pigment ink pad (gray)

felt-tip markers (several colors)

craft knife

scissors

double-sided mounting tape

Making Dimensional Cards

Pop-up cards are so fun to make and even more fun to give, appealing to adults as much as they do to kids. These dimensional cards do not take long to construct, especially if you keep a few premade parts on hand. This particular design is perfect to cut and store. Keep the stamped images simple and large—because the card itself is so impressive, you don't need to overdo it with a complex stamp!

1 If necessary, mount your stamps onto balsa wood blocks (see page 77, steps 1–2, for further instruction). Ink the image stamp with felt-tip markers, then press the stamp onto a sheet of white cardstock. Cut out the stamped image with scissors. Edge the paper with a marker.

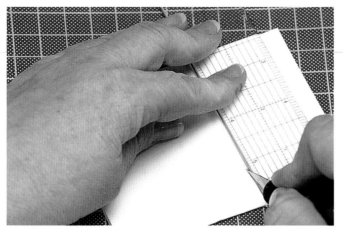

2 Trim the white A2 card to 3½" x 4¾" (9cm x 12cm). With a craft knife, cut two parallel 1" (3cm) lines, each intersecting the folded center at a 90° angle. The lines should be placed in the middle of the fold, about ½" (13mm) apart from each other.

3 Using the back of the craft knife tip, score a straight line from the top of one of the cut lines to the top of the other.

4 Open up the card. Push the pop-up center to the inside of the card.

5 Use chalk pigment ink to stamp the inside of the card, creating a patterned background design.

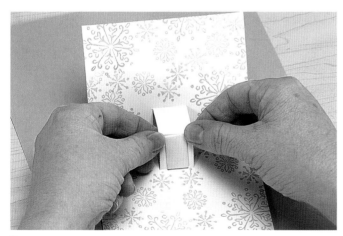

6 Apply a piece of double-sided mounting tape to the bottom half of the pop-up slot in the center. Attach the trimmed image to the tape, lining up the bottom of the image with the scored, folded line on the bottom of the slot. When you open the card, the image should pop up; when you close the card, the image should lie flat.

7 Attach the card to the inside of a colored A2 card using double-sided tape. This will provide a ¼" (6mm) border around the inside and a decorative cover on the outside.

white coated matte cardstock | JUDIKINS MATTEKOTE |

colored (light blue) A2 card

stamp | HERO ARTS DOUBLE FLOWER DESIGN |

alcohol-based inks (blue and black) | PIÑATA COLORS
OR ADIRONDACK ALCOHOL INKS |

oil-based metallic paint marker (gold)

paper towels

water spritzer, filled with rubbing alcohol

scissors

double-sided tape

tip Coated cardstock works well for this technique because its slick surface makes it easy to manipulate the inks.

Creating Faux Finishes

Looking for an excuse to experiment with your stamping stuff? Try faux finishes! Any dye-based ink will work for this technique, but I specifically used alcohol-based ink for this particular project. Alcohol-based inks are great fun for faux finishes. On coated paper stock, they dry very quickly but remain shiny, giving the surface a marble-like finish. These inks can also be used on a wide range of surfaces, like glass, plastics and metal. The metallic look of the markers adds a touch of drama and elegance.

1 Apply several drops of ink onto a sheet of coated matte cardstock, then buff the ink with a paper towel. The ink will dry very quickly. After the first layer of ink is dry, gradually add more colors, allowing each layer of ink to dry before adding another. To keep you from adding too much color, apply the ink light to dark.

2 Spritz the surface of the cardstock with alcohol.

3 Blot the surface with a paper towel, then let it dry.

4 Shake an oil-based metallic paint marker over the card-stock to spatter the surface with paint . Let the paint dry.

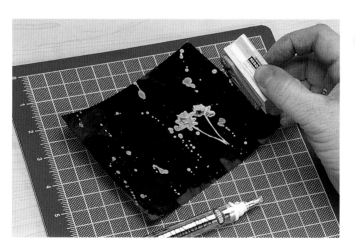

5 Ink the stamp with the metallic paint marker, then press the stamp onto the paper. Allow the paint to dry.

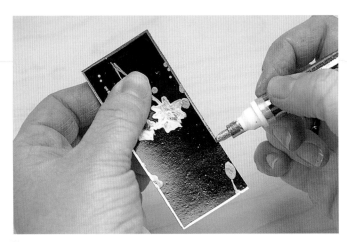

6 Trim the edges around the stamped image to form a long, vertical rectangle.

7 Edge the rectangle with the paint marker.

8 Using double-sided tape, attach the trimmed image to the remaining cardstock.

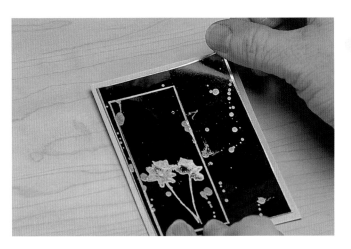

9 Adhere the layered design to the front of a colored A2 card with double-sided tape.

white coated matte cardstock | JUDIKINS MATTEKOTE |

colored (ochre) cardstock, folded into card

stamp | HERO ARTS DOUBLE FLOWER DESIGN |

alcohol-based inks (several colors) | PIÑATA COLORS

OR ADIRONDACK ALCOHOL INKS |

solvent ink pad (black)

oil-based metallic paint marker (gold)

paper towels

water spritzer, filled with rubbing alcohol

scissors

double-sided tape

Another Fun Technique

DRIPPING AND DRIZZLING INK IS ANOTHER WAY TO CREATE TEXTURE ON A SLICK SURFACE. The abstract look created by this technique can give your card a contemporary flair.

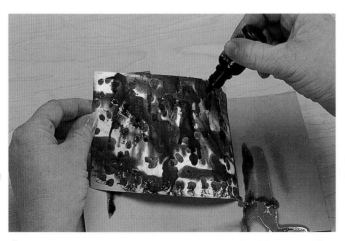

1 Spatter a sheet of coated matte cardstock with a metallic oil-based marker. Spritz with alcohol to saturate the surface. Add some alcohol-based ink while the marker is still wet, letting it run down the paper.

2 Add another color of alcohol-based ink. Blot with a paper towel and let the ink dry completely. Stamp a design on the surface with black solvent ink. Trim the design as desired and add to the front of a card.

white coated matte cardstock | JUDIKINS MATTEKOTE |

colored (brown) cardstock, folded into card

stamp | HERO ARTS DOUBLE FLOWER DESIGN |

dye inks (yellow, blue and red)

solvent ink pad (black)

metallic powdered pigments (gold) | PEARL EX |

small, stiff brush

paper towel

water spritzer, filled with rubbing alcohol

scissors

double-sided tape

Creating Faux Finishes with Powdered Pigments

Because powdered pigments are such a versatile material, you can experiment to find new and unusual ways to incorporate them into your stamping projects. If you like the look of the faux finishes created in the previous pages, give this technique a try. When added to the dye ink and alcohol mixture, powdered pigments enhance the surface with a beautiful metallic sheen. Your glowing surface will provide a beautiful background for any stamped design.

1 Spritz a sheet of coated matte cardstock with alcohol until the surface is very shiny. Add light-colored dye ink to the surface, then spread and blot the ink with a small, stiff brush.

2 Sprinkle metallic powdered pigment onto the surface and spread with a small, stiff brush.

3 Add drops of darker-colored dye ink onto the surface and spritz with alcohol.

4 Add another color of dye ink and spritz with alcohol, allowing the ink to run and create a design. Let the ink dry completely, then stamp a design on the surface with black solvent ink. Trim the design as desired and add to the front of a card.

Materials

small precut box (red)

doily

color copy of photograph

four miniature spools

stamp | HERO ARTS FLOWER DESIGN |

dye ink pad (dark purple)

dimensional glue | DIAMOND GLAZE |

felt-tip marker (red)

letter stickers and other small embellishments, such as ribbons and miniature flowers

scissors

double-sided tape

double-sided mounting tape

glue stick

Using Embellishments

Many stamp stores today have die-cut boxes, tags and cards that are easy to assemble for gifts and greetings. Little boxes are especially handy for making charming miniature shrines like this project. This is a good way to use those embellishments you've collected throughout the years. Sometimes the perfect embellishment is hidden away in a junk drawer, a sewing box or in the garage, so take a few moments to dig through your own home for small treasures that can be used to dress up cards.

1 Ink the stamp with dye ink, then press the stamp onto the unfolded box in a random design.

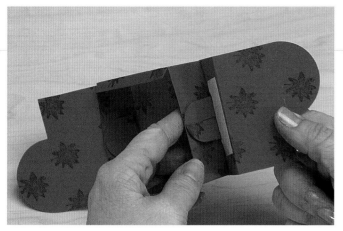

2 Fold the edges and assemble the box. Use double-sided tape to adhere the two side flaps to the base of the box.

3 Trim the doily to fit inside the box. Use a glue stick to apply glue to the back of the doily, then adhere it to the interior bottom of the box.

4 Add double-sided mounting tape to the back of a color copy of an old photograph, then adhere it to the inside of the box, placing it on top of the doily.

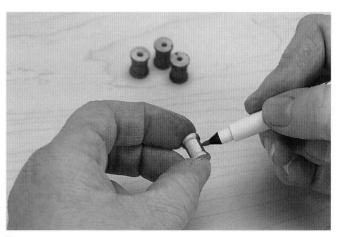

5 Color four miniature spools with a felt-tip marker to match the box.

6 Give the box four "feet" by using dimensional glue to attach the spools to the bottom of the box, placing one in each corner.

7 Add some letter stickers and any other embellishments to give the shrine a finishing touch.

Resources/ Stamp Credits

STAMP COMPANIES

American Art Stamp
3870 Del Amo Boulevard
Suite 501
Torrance, CA 90503
(310) 371-6593
www.americanartstamp.com
{stamps}

Appaloosa Art Stamps
P.O. Box 85
Viola, ID 83872
(866) 882-0333
www.aasimagick.com
{stamps}

Apropos Art Stamps and Papers
3030 South Grand Boulevard
Spokane, WA 99202
(509) 624-1754
www.aproposartstamps.com

Art Gone Wild!/Alias Smith and Rowe
3110 Payne Avenue
Cleveland, OH 44114
(800) 945-3980
www.agwstamps.com
{stamps}

JudiKins
17803 South Harvard Blvd.
Gardena, CA 90248
(310) 515-1115
www.judikins.com
{stamps, MatteKote, Diamond Glaze}

Hero Arts
1343 Powell Street
Emeryville, CA 94608
(800) 822-4376
www.heroarts.com
{stamps}

Postmodern Design
P.O. Box 720416
Norman, OK 73070
e-mail: Postmoderndesign@aol.com
{stamps}

Post Script Studio/Carmen's Veranda
P.O. Box 1539
Placentia, CA 92871
(714) 528-4529
www.postscriptstudio.com
{stamps}

Rubbermoon Stamp Company
P.O. Box 3258
Hayden Lake, ID 83835
(208) 772-9772
www.rubbermoon.com
{stamps}

A Stamp In The Hand Co.
20507 South Belshaw Avenue
Carson, CA 90746
(310) 884-9700
www.astampinthehand.com
{stamps}

SUPPLIES

AMACO
6060 Guion Road
Indianapolis, IN 46254
(800) 374-1600
www.amaco.com
{metal sheets}

Appaloosa Art
{presanded glass tiles}

Ranger Industries, Inc.
15 Park Road
Tinton Falls, NJ 07724
(800) 244-2211
www.rangerink.com
{ink pads, embossing powders and more}

Speedball Art Products Company
2226 Speedball Road
Statesville, NC 28677
(800) 898-7224
www.speedballart.com
{carving supplies}

Staedtler
21900 Plummer Street
Chatsworth, CA 91311
www.staedtler-usa.com
{crayons, markers, pencils, cutting mats,
carving blocks}

Tsukineko, Inc.
17640 NE 65th Street
Redmond, WA 98052
(800) 769-6633
www.tsukineko.com
{inks and pens}

USArtQuest, Inc.
7800 Ann Arbor Road
Grass Lake, MI 49240
(800) 200-7848
www.usartquest.com
{Piñata Colors, Pearl Ex}

Index

Create extraordinary art with rubber stamps and more!

Creative Stamping with Mixed Media Techniques

Make your rubber stamp art more colorful, unique and beautiful! Inside you'll find 20 simple recipes that combine sponging, glazing and masking techniques with colorful stamped patterns. Try them out on the 13 step-by-step projects, including a fabric wall hanging, wooden tray, flowerpot, paper lantern, journals, boxes and more.

ISBN 1-58180-347-8, paperback, 128 pages, #32315-K

Rubber Stamp Extravaganza

Use rubber stamps to decorate candles, jewelry, purses, book covers, wall hangings and more. 16 step-by-step projects show you how by using creative techniques, surfaces and embellishments, including metal, beads, embossing powder and clay—even shrink plastic!

ISBN 1-58180-128-9, paperback, 128 pages, #31829-K

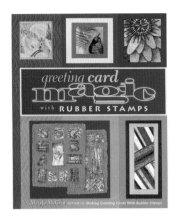

Greeting Card Magic with Rubber Stamps

Discover great new tricks for creating extra-special greeting cards! Pick up your stamp, follow along with the illustrated, step-by-step directions inside, and—*ta da!*—you'll amaze everyone (including yourself!) with your beautiful and original creations.

ISBN 0-89134-979-0, paperback, 128 pages, #31521-K

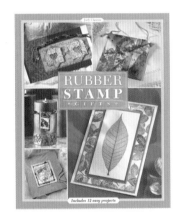

Rubber Stamp Gifts

Create rubber stamp masterpieces perfect for gift-giving any time of year! From jewelry boxes and travel journals to greeting cards and candles, Judy Claxton shows you how to make 15 gorgeous projects using easy-to-find materials and simple techniques, such as embellishing, embossing, direct to paper, paper clay, polymer clay and shrink plastic.

ISBN 1-58180-466-0, paperback, 48 pages, #32723-K

30 Minute Rubber Stamp Workshop

Let Sandra McCall show you how to make gorgeous rubber stamp treasures in 30 minutes or less. From home décor and party favors to desk accessories and wearable gifts, you'll find 27 exciting projects inside. Each one is easy to do and inexpensive to make—perfect for those days when you want to create something quick!

ISBN 1-58180-271-4, paperback, 128 pages, #32142-K

These books and other fine North Light titles are available from your local art & craft retailer, bookstore, online supplier or by calling 1-800-448-0915.